Precision
Woods and Long Iron Shots

Precision Golf
SERIES

DANIEL McDONALD

with
Richard A. Goodman

Human Kinetics

Library of Congress Cataloging-in-Publication Data

McDonald, Daniel, 1945-
    Precision woods and long iron shots / by Daniel McDonald with
Richard A. Goodman.
        p.   cm. -- (Precision golf series)
    ISBN 0-88011-766-4
    1. Golf.   2. Golf--Drive.   3. Swing (Golf)   I. Goodman, Richard
A. (Richard Alan), 1949-   . II. Title. III. Series.
GV965.M337   1998
796.352'33--DC21   97-47390
                                                        CIP
                                                        r98

ISBN: 0-88011-766-4

Copyright © 1998 by Daniel McDonald and Richard A. Goodman

Acquisitions Editor: Martin Barnard; **Developmental Editors:** Kirby Mittelmeier and Laura Casey Mast; **Assistant Editors:** Jennifer Stallard and Cynthia McEntire; **Editorial Assistant:** Laura Seversen; **Copyeditor:** Robert R. Replinger; **Proofreader:** Kirby Mittelmeier; **Graphic Designers:** Judy Henderson and Keith Blomberg; **Graphic Artist:** Kathleen Boudreau-Fuoss; **Photo Editor:** Boyd LaFoon, **Cover Designer:** Jack Davis; **Photographer (cover):** GolfStock/Pete Marovich; **Photographer (interior):** Barbara J. Rowland; **Illustrator:** Keith Blomberg; **Printer:** United Graphics

Human Kinetics books are available at special discounts for bulk purchase. Special editions or book excerpts can also be created to specification. For details, contact the Special Sales Manager at Human Kinetics.

Printed in the United States of America   10 9 8 7 6 5 4 3 2 1

Human Kinetics
Web site: http://www.humankinetics.com/

United States: Human Kinetics, P.O. Box 5076, Champaign, IL 61825-5076
1-800-747-4457
e-mail: humank@hkusa.com

Canada: Human Kinetics, Box 24040, Windsor, ON N8Y 4Y9
1-800-465-7301 (in Canada only)
e-mail: humank@hkcanada.com

Europe: Human Kinetics, P.O. Box IW14, Leeds LS16 6TR, United Kingdom
(44) 1132 781708
e-mail: humank@hkeurope.com

Australia: Human Kinetics, 57A Price Avenue, Lower Mitcham, South Australia 5062
(088) 277 1555
e-mail: humank@hkaustralia.com

New Zealand: Human Kinetics, P.O. Box 105-231, Auckland 1
(09) 523 3462
e-mail: humank@hknewz.com

Contents

Introduction

It is often said that golfers should "Drive for show, and putt for dough." Despite the merit of this statement, most amateur golfers are unable to make effective use of their longer distance clubs, so they deny themselves the chance to putt for birdies or eagles. Instead, they frequently are in the woods slashing their balls back into play, or standing on the bank of a water hazard fishing to retrieve yet another three-dollar golf ball. For these golfers, the measure of 1-under or 3-over has nothing to do with score—it but merely indicates how many golf balls they have lost or found! Even many low handicappers sabotage their rounds by unnecessarily landing their long-distance shots in the rough, bunkers, and hazards.

Without realizing it, the average amateur golfer has developed a game based on mediocre ball-striking skills and poor strategy—or even worse, no strategy at all. As a result, he believes that he is doomed to play at his current level, whether it be in the 100s, 90s, 80s, or 70s. He spends most of his time at driving ranges and golf courses merely hitting balls and not practicing effectively. So he searches the shelves of the local golf store hoping to discover the miracle driver (the so-called self-shooter), while subconsciously convinced that this is a game he will never master.

It doesn't have to be this way. Each golfer has the capacity to tame those monster par 3s, the unreachable par 4s, and the devilish par 5s. What he really needs is a good plan and sound drills to produce consistent results—drills that teach him how to produce solid contact, control, and power with all his long clubs, from the 3 iron to the driver. The combination of skill, planning, and renewed confidence can transform an erratic and frustrating game to one of poise, power, and control in any situation.

This book will provide the reader with the means to develop the skills necessary to control the flight of the ball and produce consistent distance. For advanced players, the goal is to maximize distance and placement to create birdie opportunities; for good club players, to eliminate double bogies; and for intermediate and beginning players, to eliminate fear of the tee, develop consistent ball flight, and establish a consistent swing. To achieve these goals, we outline a systematic approach in chapter 1 for you to assess your skills with woods and long irons, and to select the most appropriate club for a given situation. Chapters 2 through 6 address the full spectrum of everyday shotmaking situations calling for the driver, fairway woods, or long irons. These chapters describe simple and sound strategies for playing through each of these situations and detail drills for improving your skills with these clubs. To ensure a consistent and familiar approach, each situation includes the same basic elements of theory, application, and execution. For each situation, we have outlined the principal strategy and technique for success and described and illustrated a drill for mastering the skills necessary to handle the situation.

You can practice these drills at driving ranges and golf courses. With few exceptions, they require nothing more than dedication, imagination, and your clubs. Some of the drills may require you to have tees of varying sizes, striped range balls, and markers and targets at distances of 175 to 250 yards. Although we present most of the situations in a generic manner, irrespective of the handedness of the golfer, descriptions of the most common ball flight patterns—fades, slices, draws, and hooks—are written from the viewpoint of right-handed golfers.

By using the suggested strategies and regularly practicing the recommended drills, you will develop more effective and satisfying use of your woods and long irons, as well as greater confidence on the golf course.

Chapter 1

Assessing Your Skills

Knowing how far you can hit the ball with specific woods and long irons is critical if you want to improve your shotmaking and execute strategies appropriate for specific situations. Most golfers, however, tend to choose clubs for a specific distance or situation based not on accurate data but on euphoric recall. For the same reason, most golfers are likely to overestimate their distance capabilities with specific clubs, thereby overlooking the hazards and conditions of the moment—bunkers, water, sidehill lie, and wind. Hoping to meet unrealistic expectations for distance, golfers tend to swing too hard and too fast, thereby producing poor contact, badly misdirected shots, and penalty strokes.

Golfers also may be oblivious to gaps in their long game. For example, many players have an aversion to using the long irons. This dislike may create gaps of up to 25 yards between the shortest fairway wood and the longest iron they are comfortable hitting. For most golfers, this is the 5 iron. These gaps leave golfers with no alternative but to attempt to produce too much distance with a short club or to finesse a longer club. The problem is further compounded when golfers venture away from their home courses. Although they may be able to tailor their clubs to fit the specific conditions of their primary courses, they are often unprepared when they face different shotmaking requirements on other courses. Even golf courses of identical length and slope are likely to present radically different requirements for tee shots, second shots, and par-3 considerations.

The primary purpose of this chapter is to help you identify your strengths and weaknesses with woods and long irons. This will allow you to make the sound club selection decisions necessary for successful implementation of your course strategies. By knowing your strengths, weaknesses, and capabilities with woods and long irons, you will be able to remain calm and confident on any golf course. Developing a "club chart" that accurately lists your average distances for each club is the first step toward eliminating gaps in your game. Besides developing a club chart, you should take several additional steps to eliminate gaps in your game: analyze and define your trajectory; select the combination of clubs that maximizes your strengths and compensates for your weaknesses; maintain an accurate record of distances for your current preferred clubs; and periodically consult a qualified professional about your swing mechanics, the status of your equipment, and your plan for correcting flaws and practicing.

Create a Club Chart

By maintaining a record of your shotmaking on a chart, you can establish a realistic and accurate benchmark for shotmaking. To create the chart, document for each club in your bag both the distance you carry a typical shot and the distance the shot rolls on a level surface. Determine these distances by collecting data during practice and play over a month, including three to five sessions at a driving range and one to three rounds on a golf course. Take an average of your figures. See the sample club chart (table 1.1, page 4) as an example, and use the uncompleted chart for your data (table 1.2, page 5).

This data may often reveal important flaws in your club selection. In addition, the information may highlight the point at which you begin to lose a consistent differential in distance with your different clubs. For example, for higher-lofted irons the average differential may be 10 yards, while for longer irons the differential may diminish to 5 yards. The change in differential may reflect factors such as variation in the loft or lie of the clubs, weakening of the shafts, stiffness of the shafts, or a fundamental swing flaw. As you use the club chart to compare the loft characteristics of long irons and fairway woods, you may discover that you are losing distance with your long irons but that the loft characteristics of the 4 wood adequately meet your distance requirements. To help you fill in the gaps, the loft and lie of many of these clubs can be adjusted. You can obtain information about loft and lie for your clubs from the manufacturer or from many club repair professionals.

Analyze Your Trajectories

The natural shot trajectory of each golfer is unique and ranges from very low (the "low-ball hitter" as exemplified by Lee Trevino) to very high (the "high-ball hitter" as exemplified by Greg Norman). By knowing your trajectory characteristics, you will be able to make the correct decisions about club selection and strategy in all situations. For example, if you are naturally a low-ball hitter and you are trying to increase the trajectory in a long shot, then you may opt to use your 4 wood instead of your 1 iron because you can more easily produce a higher-trajectory shot with this club. On the other hand, if you are a hitter who "hits it high and lets it fly," you would not want to use a 12 degree shallow-faced driver because it tends to add even more loft to a shot you want to hit lower to increase both the roll and total distance.

Select the Right Combination of Clubs

Because of the varying conditions and requirements of different golf courses, as well as the limitations imposed by the 14-club rule, you must be able to select the combination of clubs that maximizes your strengths and compensates for your weaknesses. On a weekly basis, top professionals and amateur players alike must choose the 14 clubs that enhance their scoring potential for a given golf course. Many of these players possess drivers of varying lofts—from 7 to 12 degrees of loft—and additional fairway woods. Effective use of the data that you maintain on your club chart will help you to make choices that will lower your score.

Maintain an Accurate Record

The combination of technological advances in golf equipment and improvements in your game as the result of practice will change your distances and club preferences. Therefore, you will need to update your club chart at least annually to maintain its accuracy. Documenting your performance will also help you pinpoint your practice needs.

Obtain an Objective Assessment

The final critical step for eliminating gaps in your game is to consult a qualified professional periodically to obtain an objective assessment of your swing mechanics and the status of your equipment. The pro can also develop a plan for correcting your flaws and practicing. This objective assessment will eliminate guesswork about your game, saving you time and making your practice more effective and your play more rewarding.

Club	Length (inches)	Loft (degrees)	Shaft (G, S)	Flex (F, R)	Carry (yards)	Roll (yards)	Total (yards)
Driver	44	9	G	F	225	15	240
3 wood	43	16	G	F	205	15	220
4 wood	42.5	19	G	F	195	10	205
5 wood	41.5	22	G	F	190	10	200
7 wood	41.5	28	G	F	175	10	185
1 iron	39.5	16	S	R	200	10-15	210-215
2 iron	39	19	S	R	190	10	200
3 iron	38.5	22	S	R	180	10	190
4 iron	38	28	S	R	170	10	180
5 iron	37.5	32	S	R	160	10	170
6 iron	37	36	S	R	150	10	160
7 iron	36.5	40	S	R	140	8	148
8 iron	36	44	S	R	130	6	136
9 iron	35.5	48	S	R	120	5	125
P-wedge	35	50	S	R	100	5	105
S-wedge	35	56	S	R	70	0-5	70-75
L-wedge	35	60	S	R	0-50	0-5	0-55

Table 1.1   Sample Club Chart

KEY: **G**—Graphite, **S**—Steel, **F**—Firm, **R**—Regular

Club	Length (inches)	Loft (degrees)	Shaft (G, S)	Flex (F, R)	Carry (yards)	Roll (yards)	Total (yards)
Driver							
3 wood							
4 wood							
5 wood							
7 wood							
1 iron							
2 iron							
3 iron							
4 iron							
5 iron							
6 iron							
7 iron							
8 iron							
9 iron							
P-wedge							
S-wedge							
L-wedge							

Table 1.2 Blank Club Chart

KEY: **G**—Graphite, **S**—Steel, **F**—Firm, **R**—Regular

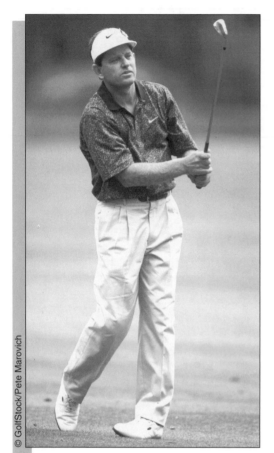

© GolfStock/Pete Marovich

Nick Price:
The Total Driver

To play golf at the level of the PGA Tour, you must be able to drive the ball with both consistent distance and accuracy. The main statistic that separates the upper and lower tiers of players on the mens PGA Tour is the percentage of fairways hit per round (fairways hit is defined as those on which the drive lands and comes to rest within the confines of the fairway). The leader in total driving—which is a combination of the rank in distance per drive and the number of fairways hit per round—almost always ranks among the top ten Tour money winners each year.

Nick Price's meteoric rise on the Tour paralleled his mastery of the driver. Price climbed from a ranking of 97th in driving distance in 1990 to a ranking of 6th in 1994. During the same period, he also improved his driving accuracy, moving from a ranking of 49th to 37th, hitting nearly three-quarters of fairways in regulation. In 1994, because of the combination of his driving distance and accuracy, he attained the rank of number 1 for total driving and became the number 1-ranked player in the world with earnings of $1.5 million. This mastery of the driver also aided in his seven U.S. Tour wins during this period, including two majors—the PGA Championship and the British Open.

Price learned the fundamentals of golf in Zimbabwe and South Africa, and has played the professional tours in the United States and in Europe since 1979. While he currently resides in Orlando, Florida, he continues to play worldwide and is ranked among the leaders on the Tour. At a moderate height of only 5'10" and weight of approximately 160 pounds, Price nonetheless consistently produces drives of prodigious distance and exceptional accuracy—shots that average nearly 278 yards per drive.

Chapter 2

Driver From the Tee

The first chapter provided you with a framework and tips for determining how far you are currently hitting specific woods and long irons. This chapter focuses on using the driver from the tee box. Effective use of the driver is one of the three basic skills necessary for playing successful golf (the other two are putting and wedge play). The situations and drills in this chapter are grouped into three basic categories: those that require the most basic and solid shots (situations 1-4), those that require curved shots (situations 5-10), and those posing special demands or opportunities (situations 11-13). By starting with the basic situations and drills presented in situations 1-4—situations that include hitting your driver to a generous fairway, uphill, downhill, or over water—you will begin to develop the habits of good alignment, posture, and ball position. By correctly applying the basic techniques in these situations, you will maximize your weight transfer and make the solid contact necessary to achieve your full distance potential with the driver.

To become proficient with the driver from the tee box, you must be able to curve the ball in certain situations. Common situations requiring this ability include tee shots to doglegs (both right and left) and to fairways bordered by out-of-bounds or by lateral water hazards. Situations 5-10 present these conditions. The accompanying techniques and drills will help you learn how to curve your tee shots effectively. The drills for these situations emphasize the importance of being aware of your specific target and develop skills for aiming these shots.

Finally, situations 11-13 pose special demands or opportunities, including hitting the driver to a heavily bunkered fairway, from a tree-lined chute, or to a reachable par 4. The drills in these situations will help you achieve optimal control, a full and fluid swing, and maximum distance potential under the right circumstances.

The conditions described in situations 5-10 require you to hit curved shots with consistency, accuracy, and confidence. These situations call for shots conventionally termed controlled fades, controlled draws, power fades, power draws, controlled slices, and controlled hooks. Before you attempt to practice the techniques for these shots, you need a clear understanding of the concepts and geometry underlying the terms. A controlled fade and a controlled draw with the driver are shots that curve 10 to 15 yards from a straight line that bisects the fairway from the midpoint of the tee box to the midpoint of the landing area. The power fade and the power draw increase the total distance of a shot, while at the same time delaying the occurrence of the curve. The controlled hook and controlled slice will double the amount of the curve to approximately 15 to 30 yards. Use an open stance to produce a controlled fade or controlled slice, and use a closed stance to produce a controlled draw or controlled hook. Situations 5 and 6 detail the basic technique, geometry, and alignment factors necessary to be successful with these shots.

The drills contained in this chapter define the basic building blocks for correct swing technique and consistency. The most important of these are detailed in situations 1, 5, and 6. You will need to be both comfortable and conversant with these techniques before you begin to tackle many of the situations in other chapters. In a sense, these techniques and associated drills are like prerequisites for an advanced course. Therefore, you will want to revisit these situations periodically and practice the drills regularly at the range and on the course.

© Nabisco Dinah Shore

Lisolette Neumann:
Master of the Fairway Woods

LPGA Tour star Lisolette Neumann, while ranking only average in the length of drives (ranked 57th in 1996), is renowned for her mastery of the fairway woods. Her ability to consistently utilize these clubs with maximum effectiveness increases her options from both the tee and fairway on virtually all par 4s and par 5s. Trademarks of Neumann's use of these clubs are her grace and tempo which combine to produce a seemingly effortless swing. Because most of the major championships on the LPGA Tour are played on long and demanding courses, Neumann's mastery of the fairway woods has allowed her to win one U.S. Open and to remain a contender in all major championships.

Neumann was born in Fingspang, Sweden, in 1966, and has played the U.S. LPGA tour for nine years. She has notched eight Tour victories and one major championship. In 1994, she was honored by *Golf World* as the Most Improved Player. She was also named Swedish Player of the Year. Neumann was a member of the Solheim Cup European Team in 1990, 1992, 1994, and 1996. Her career earnings on the LPGA Tour are $2.3 million, ranking her as the 16th all-time money winner among women professionals. Compared with other women on the professional tour, Neumann carries an unusually large number of fairway woods.

1 Straight to an Open Fairway

SITUATION: A tee shot at a distance of 225 to 260 yards to a generous fairway. The landing area is 50 yards wide with no bunkers or hazards.

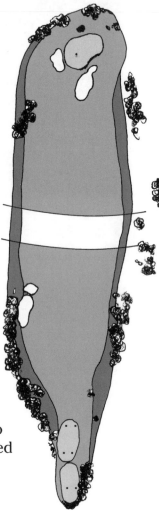

STRATEGY:

Make an aggressive full swing with the driver, focusing especially on weight transfer, club head speed, and balance—factors essential for maximum transfer of energy to the ball and therefore essential for maximum distance. Aim to a target the size of a blanket in the center of the fairway.

TECHNIQUE:

Tee the ball so that its center is even with the top of the club face (see photo a). Stand with feet shoulder-width apart (that is, the separation of the insteps of the feet should equal the width of the shoulders) with the classic bend at the waist, pendulum placement of the arms, flexed knees, and even distribution of weight on both feet. Position the ball two and one-half to three inches inside the forward heel.

CONCEPT:

An aggressive, full swing with the driver requires balance, rhythm, and tempo to produce power and accuracy. These factors help you maintain a full and proper swing arc by allowing the club head to accelerate to maximum speed. This concept also eliminates the need to overcontrol, or guide, your swing.

DRILL:

This drill's objective is to promote full weight transfer as part of finishing the swing. Take a full stance, but place the ball three to four inches ahead of its normal position, or even outside the forward foot. Make a full swing, aggressively moving through the hitting zone and finishing high and in balance (see photo b). Your forward arm should make a 90-degree angle at your elbow, and your thumbs should point over your shoulder or behind your head. Hold the finish a full 10 seconds to achieve complete balance.

Straight to an Open Fairway

a

b

TIP: If you feel yourself guiding your club through the swing, close your eyes and make several practice swings. Focus on sensing the weight in the club head as it brushes grass at the bottom of the swing—a sensation similar to twirling a rock or other heavy object attached to a string. Your ability to sense the club head indicates that you have transferred energy properly and have not forced or overcontrolled the club during the forward swing.

2 Uphill Fairway

SITUATION: A tee shot steeply uphill to a landing area at a distance of 225 to 250 yards.

STRATEGY:

Make solid contact to allow use of all available loft on the driver, producing sufficient carry to reach the top of the hill.

TECHNIQUE:

Use the basic stance and tee the ball at its normal height (see situation 1, page 10).

CONCEPT:

Avoid attempting to help the ball into the air by pulling up or away from the ball. This frequently results in a low, sculled shot into the hill. In addition, maintain the fundamental commitment to good posture and to weight transfer to the forward foot at the bottom of the swing.

DRILL:

The purpose of this drill is to help you avoid the tendency to pull up by developing the habit of maintaining good posture through and beyond the moment of impact. Use the basic stance and ball position, and place a second tee three to four inches in front of the ball and tee (see photo a). Your swing should clip both tees from the ground (see photo b).

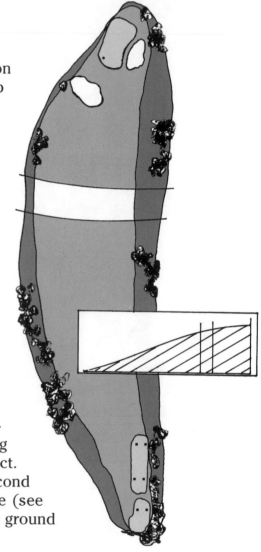

a

b

TIP: Focus on the second tee and on maintaining your posture throughout impact with the ball.

3 Downhill Fairway

SITUATION: A tee shot over a long, gradual decline to a landing area at a distance of 225 to 260 yards.

STRATEGY:

Make a swing with good rhythm, tempo, and balance (see situation 1, page 10).

TECHNIQUE:

Narrow the stance by moving your back foot closer to your forward foot, leaving a separation of the heels of 8 to 10 inches; the ball position should be normal relative to your forward foot (see photo a).

CONCEPT:

Because most golfers are always in pursuit of the longest possible drive (approximately 300 yards), downhill tee shots tempt golfers to overswing in hopes of achieving greater distance. Narrowing the stance counters this tendency by ensuring a slower, more rhythmic swing. A slower swing is desirable because it can improve weight transfer and produce more solid contact between the club head and ball.

DRILL:

Use the narrow stance and a driver with an extremely flexible shaft (for example, a Maltzie Easy Swinger) to slow your swing while hitting practice shots. The exaggerated flexibility of the shaft requires extremely slow swing speed and passive hands. Do not focus on using your hands to help guide the club through the impact area of the forward swing. You will know you have executed this drill correctly when you can consistently hit a draw or slight hook.

a

TIP: Attempt to swing at one-half normal speed with extra relaxation in your arms.

4 Over Water

SITUATION: A tee shot that must carry over water (for example, a pond or small lake) to a flat, wide landing area at a distance of at least 180 yards.

STRATEGY:

Hit a full, solid tee shot that carries a minimum of 200 yards in the air.

TECHNIQUE:

This shot requires a full swing and basic stance (see situation 1, page 10) but with approximately two-thirds of your weight set behind the ball on your back foot.

CONCEPT:

Most golfers become tense when confronted by large water hazards, diminishing their ability to make a full and fluid swing. Therefore, make a full swing with an emphasis on a full shoulder turn (that is, turn your back completely to the target) and weight transfer in both the back and forward swings to achieve the maximum power potential in this situation.

DRILL:

This drill will help you see the golf ball from the correct position at the top of the backswing. A tense golfer shortens the backswing, his head and eyes directly above the ball, causing a reverse weight transfer in which the weight finishes on the back foot at the end of the swing. Use the basic stance and ball position (see situation 1, page 10), but place two-thirds of your weight on your back foot. Place a second ball four to six inches behind and outside the target line of the primary ball (see photo a). Focus on the second ball during the take away to ensure proper weight transfer to your back foot and to allow your head to remain four to six inches behind the ball at the top of the backswing. Looking directly at the second ball, use peripheral vision to see the primary ball (see photo b). You will develop the habit of seeing the back of the ball, that is, seeing the ball from the swinging position. Complete the swing with normal tempo and follow-through. As you practice this drill, you will notice that at the top of the backswing you can see both balls at the same time.

a

b

TIP: To avoid the tendency to fixate on the water hazard during practice and play, focus on a target point on or above the horizon.

5 Dogleg Right

SITUATION: A tee shot to a generous fairway with a right dogleg. The landing area is at a distance of 225 to 250 yards, and bunkers guard the right-hand corner.

STRATEGY:

Hit the tee shot from left to right by using a controlled fade. This will allow use of the entire fairway for landing the shot. A controlled fade is a tee shot that curves from left to right approximately 10 to 15 yards.

TECHNIQUE:

Take an open stance by creating an angle of 25 to 30 degrees to the left of the intended target line by moving the body line (your feet, hips, and shoulders) 25 to 30 degrees to the left of the target line. Move the ball forward one and a half inches. Keep the club face square to the target in the middle of the fairway; do not aim the club face to the left of the target.

CONCEPT:

Learn to use the angle created by your alignment at address to produce an outside swing path relative to the original target line. This will ensure a left-to-right shot without altering your swing. The resulting controlled fade shot closely follows the contour of the fairway.

DRILL:

Select a mat or hitting area on the far right-hand side of the practice range. Using the open stance, align yourself so that the ball starts out on a line 20 yards to the left of the boundary (for example, a fence, netting, or tree line) and then curves back to the right before coming to rest as it nears the boundary. Remember to keep the club face aimed at the target in the fairway.

a

TIP: To ensure that you follow the intended swing path, place two clubs on the ground parallel to one another but at an angle of 25 to 30 degrees to the left of the intended target line (see photo a). You can place a third club two to three feet behind the ball and on a line directed toward the target in the fairway. The club head should remain square to the intended target; on take away, the swing path should follow the outside club to produce an outside-to-inside swing path.

6 Dogleg Left

> **SITUATION:** A tee shot to the fairway of a moderate dogleg moving from right to left. The narrow landing area is at a distance of 225 to 250 yards.

STRATEGY:

A controlled hook or draw shot places the ball in the middle of the dogleg, allowing use of the entire fairway and providing the greatest potential for a successful second shot.

TECHNIQUE:

Take a closed stance by creating an angle of 25 to 30 degrees to the right of the intended target line to the middle of the fairway. Move your back foot two to three inches to the back and move the ball back one and a half inches in the stance. Keep the club face square to the target in the middle of the fairway.

CONCEPT:

Learn to use the angle created by your alignment at address to produce an inside swing path. This ensures a right-to-left shot without altering your swing. By contacting the inside corner of the ball with the club head, you produce the spin necessary for a natural draw or controlled hook shot that closely follows the contour of the fairway.

DRILL:

Select a mat or hitting area on the far left-hand side of the practice range. Using the closed stance just described and with the aid of three clubs (see situation 5, page 18), align yourself so that the ball starts out on a line 20 yards to the right of the boundary (fence, netting, or tree line). The ball should then curve back to the left before coming to rest as it nears the boundary. Set a striped range ball on the tee with the stripe oriented diagonally from the bottom left to upper right (see photo a); focus on hitting the ball on the stripe.

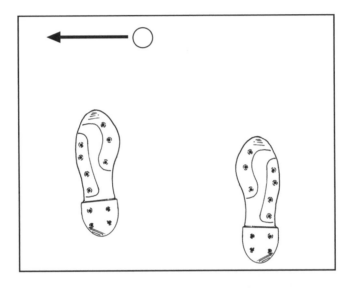

a

TIP: If you continue to hit straight or slice the ball, relax your hands and arms as you swing. Concentrate on turning your arms counterclockwise so that your forearms touch together as your hands and club reach waist-high level during follow-through.

7 **Double Dogleg**

SITUATION: A tee shot to a twisting fairway with an average width of 35 yards and a distance of 225 to 245 yards to the first dogleg.

STRATEGY:

Because the double dogleg presents a more restricted area for landing the tee shot, the full swing requires a greater emphasis on distance control and accuracy. The goal here is to preserve the maximum number of options for the next shot.

TECHNIQUE:

Make a full swing with a narrowed stance. Move the back foot closer to the center to separate the heels by 10 to 12 inches; the ball should remain in the normal position (see photo a).

CONCEPT:

Mastering the driver requires that you develop the ability to hit with control to a range of distances—175 yards, 200 yards, 225 yards, and beyond. To make successful shots to these different distances, you must be able to vary the length of the backswing and the tempo of the swing. You will need to narrow your stance slightly for the short-distance shots and widen your stance to normal width for shots of full distance (see photo b).

DRILL:

The purpose of this drill is to help you create a single axis point that will produce a slightly rounder swing path necessary for a controlled draw shot. Use the technique of the narrower stance only in practice sessions, not during play. Begin with a stance of only five or six inches separating the heels. Hit five balls, focusing on producing a swing that will carry each ball approximately 175 yards. Then increase the width of the stance by two to three inches and focus on carrying each ball 200 yards. Continue increasing the width until you have reached a normal stance (see photo b) and are making a full swing with normal tempo, hitting to your maximum distance potential and still producing a slight draw.

a

b

TIP: Because the rotation of the torso and shoulders is radically reduced by the narrower stance, you may be tempted to lift the club rather than turn your back to the target as you would in a normal swing. To avoid lifting the club during the drill, focus on keeping the club head as close to the ground as possible for the first two or three feet of the take away.

8 90-Degree Dogleg

STRATEGY:

Drive the ball all the way to the corner to obtain a full view of and an unobstructed shot to the green.

TECHNIQUE:

Begin with basic positioning of the feet and ball relative to the target line (see situation 1, page 10). Make a controlled take away by using a three-quarters backswing—place your hands in the 10 o'clock position (see photo a) and complete the swing with a full follow-through (see photo b).

CONCEPT:

The objective for this shot—placement of the ball in the opening to the green—requires you to hit a shot of maximum accuracy by minimizing the amount of curve (that is, hook or slice). Because the severity of the angle of the dogleg limits the opening to the green (see diagram), minimizing the curve of the shot will increase the likelihood that the shot will remain within the boundary of the window of opening to the green.

DRILL:

The purpose of this drill is to provide you with an exact feel for the desired length of backswing. Use the pitching wedge and driver to practice making backswings of identical length and tempo. Alternate clubs after each shot until you achieve a consistent feel for the 10 o'clock positioning of the club at the top of the backswing.

90-Degree Dogleg

a

b

TIP: Imagine you are standing in a clock and try to set your hands at the proper position at the top of your backswing.

9 Narrow Fairway With Out-of-Bounds

SITUATION: A tee shot to a narrow fairway at a distance of approximately 400 yards to the green. The left-hand side of the fairway is lined by a close out-of-bounds all the way from the tee to the green.

STRATEGY:

Hit a power fade to achieve maximum power and distance with a high degree of accuracy. This strategy permits you to use the entire fairway by moving the ball away from potential trouble areas toward the center of the fairway.

TECHNIQUE:

Take a slightly open stance (see situation 5, page 18) by creating an angle 15 to 20 degrees to the left of the target line and moving the ball forward one inch. Keep the club face square to the target in the middle of the fairway.

CONCEPT:

The correct setup will result in a full drive while still producing a slight fade or left-to-right curve of the ball.

DRILL:

Select a mat or hitting area on the far left-hand side of the practice range. Open the stance slightly to 15 to 20 degrees from the intended target line (see photo a). Start the ball out on a line as close to the left-hand boundary as possible and produce a shot that fades 10 to 15 yards to the right of the boundary (see photo b).

Narrow Fairway With Out-of-Bounds

a
b

> **TIP:** Maintain a relaxed feeling in your hands and arms by using a full preshot routine for every practice shot and attempt to feel the weight of the club head before swinging.

Fairway With Lateral Hazard

> **SITUATION:** A tee shot to a generous fairway with a length of 420 yards to the green. The entire length of the fairway is guarded by a lateral water hazard on the right-hand side.

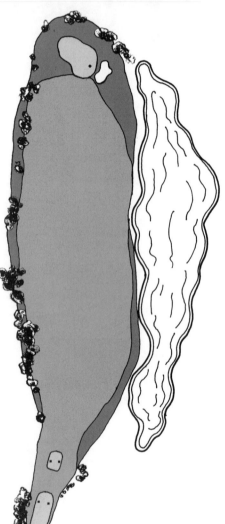

STRATEGY:

Hit a controlled draw shot (that is, a slight hook), combining full power and curving the ball away from trouble on the right to the middle of the fairway.

TECHNIQUE:

Use a slightly closed stance (see situation 6, page 20) by creating an angle of 15 to 20 degrees to the right of a straight target line to the middle of the fairway. Keep the club face square to the initial target line and move the ball back one inch in the stance toward the back foot.

CONCEPT:

The correct stance and aim will begin the ball on a line 15 to 20 yards to the left of the hazard and produce a draw that carries the ball away from the hazard toward the center of the fairway.

DRILL:

Select a mat or practice tee situated between two yardage markers, target greens, or landmarks that simulate a fairway with a width of 25 to 40 yards. Using the slightly closed stance (see photo a), practice hitting shots that begin immediately to the left of the right-hand marker, then curve to the left but remain within the confined area of the simulated fairway (see photo b).

a

b

TIP: Rotate the club face to a position where both the face of the club and the back of your forward hand are facing the ground when the club head has reached waist height during the forward swing. To ensure proper rotation of the club face through impact, make several practice swings with a feeling as though the toe end of the club is knocking the tee out of the ground and passing the heel of the club in the impact zone.

11 **Heavily Bunkered Fairway**

> **SITUATION:** A tee shot to a fairway that narrows from 40 to 25 yards and is bunkered by four to six bunkers in the landing area at a distance of approximately 225 to 245 yards

STRATEGY:

Hit a controlled, curving tee shot that eliminates bunkers on one side of the fairway in the landing area.

TECHNIQUE:

Use either the closed or open stance (see situations 5 and 6, pages 18 and 20) as appropriate to achieve maximum control.

CONCEPT:

The first step is to decide whether to hit a controlled draw or a controlled fade to the landing area. After making this decision, select the correct starting line for aiming the tee shot. Correctly aiming the shot is critical for success.

DRILL:

First, from your practice mat or tee, create an imaginary line by selecting a landmark (a flagstick, yardage sign, tree, or other stationary object). Second, aim your club face at the target and then adjust your stance and alignment for a controlled draw (see photo a) or controlled fade. And third, paying careful attention to your aim and starting line for the shot, practice shots that hook or slice around the imaginary line and landmark to the target landing area.

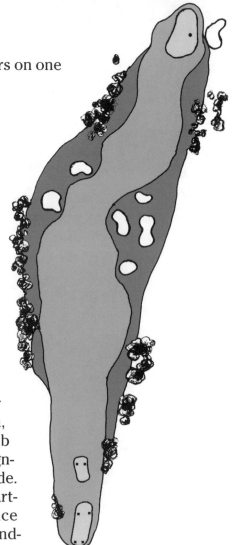

Heavily Bunkered Fairway

a

TIP: If you have difficulty hitting these shots, you may not be properly aligning your feet or stance. To ensure proper alignment, place clubs on the ground to establish the proper starting lines and swing paths.

12 Tree-Lined Chute

SITUATION: A shot from a tee recessed in a tree grove with an open chute 25 yards wide and approximately 50 yards deep before it flares to the fairway.

STRATEGY:

The confining nature of this tee shot—in proximity to trees, branches, and shrubs—causes tenseness and anxiety. To make an effective shot in this situation, you must split the chute with the initial starting line of your shot.

TECHNIQUE:

Use the basic stance and ball position (see situation 1, page 10).

CONCEPT:

In this situation golfers often try to overcontrol the swing by excessively shortening the backswing and then hurrying the forward swing. Your goal is to overcome this tendency.

DRILL:

To simulate a chute, first select a mat or practice tee close to a boundary (trees or fence) and then extend a chalk line or rope 10 to 15 yards straight ahead from the tee toward the target (see photo a). Practice hitting shots that start the ball directly above this line for the first 50 to 75 yards.

a

TIP: If you feel yourself guiding this shot with a tight, restricted arm swing, practice throwing a golf ball underhanded from a normal stance as far down the target line as possible. Then try to recreate the same feeling with your normal swing.

13 Reachable Par 4

SITUATION: A tee shot to a 275- to 300-yard par-4 hole with a generous opening to the front of the green.

STRATEGY:

Maximize your distance potential by hitting a tee shot that either flies onto or close to the green, providing an opportunity for either a birdie or an eagle.

TECHNIQUE:

In the setup, add more weight to your back foot by using the same technique as for hitting a tee shot over water (see situation 4, page 16).

CONCEPT:

Because of the temptation to reach the green, many golfers tend to overswing on this shot. Overcoming this tendency requires that you swing as though you are attempting to hit the ball only 75 percent of the distance to the green. The result of this modification will be smoother weight transfer and more solid contact—the keys to maximum distance.

DRILL:

Using a hinged-shaft Medicus Club (see photo a), practice hitting 30 or 40 tee shots without letting the club break down (that is, separating the shaft at the hinge). A breakdown of the club may indicate overuse of the hands and arms, a swing tempo of excessive speed, or a poor transition from the backswing to the forward swing.

a

b

TIP: If the Medicus Club breaks during the take away, focus on moving your shoulders, arms, hands, and club as one unit until you reach the completion point of the backswing (see photo b).

© GolfStock/Pete Marovich

Arnold Palmer:
Driving Power and Accuracy

At the 1960 U.S. Open at Cherry Hills Country Club in Denver, Arnold Palmer began the final round with no apparent hope for victory. After playing a mistake-riddled morning round, he approached the first tee of the final round six shots behind the leader. In the fashion typical of the Palmer legend, he hitched his pants, took his stance, and with one of his most powerful swings, launched a tee shot that came to rest 346 yards away on the green. This amazing shot led to an easy two-putt birdie which ignited one of the most incredible comebacks in the history of golf. For the world of golf, Palmer's extraordinary shot demonstrated the tremendous advantage to be gained by adding power to accuracy when driving the ball. Throughout Palmer's storied career, one of his trademarks was to go for broke with his drive and let the chips fall where they may—frequently producing drives of incredible distance and accuracy.

Chapter 3

Fairway Woods

This chapter presents situations requiring the use of fairway woods from both the tee and the fairway. By combining the effective use of fairway woods with the driver, you can create more opportunities for birdies and eagles on par 5s and long par 4s. Again, the club chart will provide you with accurate data for effectively matching club selection with strategies. Moreover, exact knowledge of your distance capabilities with specific clubs increases your options from the tee box on holes of moderate distance that place a premium on accuracy. By knowing your distance capabilities you will also be aware of options for using your fairway woods for the long and difficult par 3s now common on many golf courses.

The situations and drills in this chapter are again grouped into three categories. The first group of situations (situations 14-18) provides drills for managing the most common challenges, including fairway wood shots from the tee box, shots to long par 3s, and shots to an uphill or downhill green. These situations and drills will foster and reinforce your mastery of the fundamental techniques for use of the fairway woods. The second group (situations 19-22) guides you to technique adjustments and strategies necessary for handling uneven lies from the fairway. The last group (situations 23-25) addresses situations that may require curved shots and describes approaches for making successful shots from fairway bunkers.

14   From the Tee

SITUATION: A tee shot on a par-4 hole with a total distance of 390 yards from the tee to green. At a distance of 230 yards, a small creek (or other lateral hazard) causes a narrowing of the fairway to a width of approximately 15 to 20 yards.

STRATEGY:

Use the 3, 4, or 5 wood to lay up immediately short of the narrowing of the fairway.

TECHNIQUE:

Use the basic stance (see situation 1, page 10) with the ball positioned two inches inside your forward heel and your weight distributed evenly.

CONCEPT:

Two basic factors determine selection of the fairway wood for this shot: (1) the club should satisfy the specific distance requirement (205 to 220 yards), and (2) the club should produce a minimal amount of roll once the ball hits the ground.

DRILL:

This drill is intended to help you to achieve the correct launch angle for hitting a full high-trajectory fairway wood off the tee. Use the basic stance and set up and 20 or 30 striped range balls. Place a striped range ball on the tee so that the stripe is parallel with the ground and even with the top of the club face of the 3, 4, or 5 wood (see photo a). Focus on contacting the stripe on each ball with the center of the club face—you have succeeded in doing this correctly if the tee pops into the air with each shot. Contacting the ball in this manner will increase the spin, thereby reducing the roll.

a

b

TIP: If you are unable to pop the tee into the air, you may be lifting your torso at the waist. Therefore, focus especially on maintaining your posture angle at the waist at the moment of impact with the ball (see photo b).

15 Low Trajectory Shot

SITUATION: A 440-yard par-4 hole requiring a second shot of 180 to 225 yards to a large two-tiered green with the pin positioned on the back tier.

STRATEGY:

Hit a full fairway wood shot that lands on the lower tier, rolls back near the pin located on the back tier, and remains on the green.

TECHNIQUE:

To ensure that the ball releases and rolls forward after it hits the green, use a slightly lower trajectory than you would for a normal fairway wood shot. Place the ball back one to two inches in the basic stance and initially put slightly more than half your body weight on the forward foot (see photo a).

CONCEPT:

To select the proper club, you must first accurately estimate the distance from the ball placement to the front of the green. Use of the proper club ensures that you land the ball on the front tier of the green rather than yield to the temptation to fly the ball all the way to the flag.

DRILL:

The purpose of this drill is to reduce the angle of attack and delay the hit to produce a shot of low trajectory and sufficient roll. Place a series of 10 tees in a line, spacing them at intervals of three inches and leaving only the top quarter inch of each tee visible above the ground (see photo b). Using the technique just described, swing by leading with your knees, thereby controlling the bottom of the swing circle with your weight transfer. The proper technique will clip each tee out of the ground without taking a divot behind the tee.

a

b

TIP: Focus on trying to move both knees simultaneously.

16 Long Par 3

SITUATION: A tee shot to a green at a distance of 180 to 235 yards. The green opens generously on its front but is guarded by bunkers on both sides and the back.

STRATEGY:

This shot requires use of a 3, 4, or 5 wood to attain maximum trajectory at this distance. In addition, the shot should be straight to the green or drawn slightly from right to left to achieve maximum distance potential.

TECHNIQUE:

Increase the width of the basic stance by one or two inches (see situation 1, page 10) and place approximately two-thirds of your weight behind the ball on the back foot (see photo a). In the address position, set your hands even with or slightly behind the ball.

CONCEPT:

Proper execution requires good balance, a full turn of the shoulders, and complete transfer of weight from the back foot through the ball to the forward foot and finishing position. The momentum of the full release of the right side (that is, full weight transfer from the back foot to the forward foot) helps to keep the club on the target line a few inches longer and eliminates excessive side spin that causes shots to slice or hook away from the target.

DRILL:

Using the stance and technique just described, place three clubs on the ground to indicate (1) ball position, (2) target line, and (3) body line. Place the clubs parallel to the target but staggered forward (see photo b). While hitting balls, be certain that before you finish your swing, your club first reaches a point above an extension of the club that indicates the body line, and is parallel to the target line. Your swing continues to a final standard finish.

a   b

TIP: If you are pushing or pulling this shot, then imagine a chest-level finish line at a distance of five or six feet toward the target. Try to touch the finish line with the club before finishing the swing.

17 Full Swing to an Elevated Green

> **SITUATION:** A full distance shot from a fairway lie to an elevated green at a distance of 180 to 225 yards. Bunkers guard the front of the green.

STRATEGY:

Hit a shot with sufficient trajectory to carry both the hill and the bunkers guarding the front of the green.

TECHNIQUE:

Use the basic stance (see situation 1, page 10) but with two-thirds of your weight initially on the back foot.

CONCEPT:

In approaching this situation, most golfers select a club with loft insufficient to carry the hill. By using a lower-lofted club such as a 3 wood, many golfers will pull this shot to the left.

DRILL:

Place a series of 10 tees in a line, spacing them at intervals of three inches. Begin with one inch of tee visible above ground (see photo a). Clip each tee out of the ground and then reinsert each tee with three-quarters of an inch above the ground. Repeat the drill at this height and again at both one-half inch and one-quarter inch. Varying the heights of the tees requires that you maintain proper posture at several levels, while at the same time allowing the club face to find the bottom of the swing circle and elevate the ball.

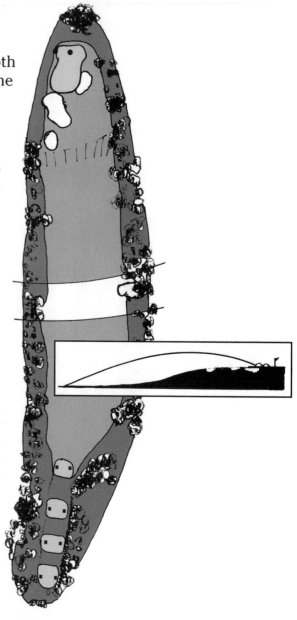

a

TIP: If you continue to top or scull the ball on these shots, then attempt to feel the elbow of your back arm maintain contact with your hip through the moment of impact.

18 Full Swing to a Green Below

SITUATION: A full shot over a long downhill slope to a green at a distance of 180 to 235 yards and lying from 30 feet to 50 feet below the initial point of the shot on the fairway.

STRATEGY:

Make an aggressive shot with increased trajectory t achieve a softer landing and carry the shot the full di: tance to the flag.

TECHNIQUE:

Use the basic stance and ball position (see situation 1 page 10), but choke down approximately one inch on th(club grip (see photo a).

CONCEPT:

Take full advantage of the terrain features in this situation—a fairway lie that is substantially higher than the green—by combining the effects of a less-lofted club and the relative gain in trajectory associated with the change in elevation. Choke down on the grip of a less-lofted fairway wood but still make an aggressive shot; the ball will land softly on the green.

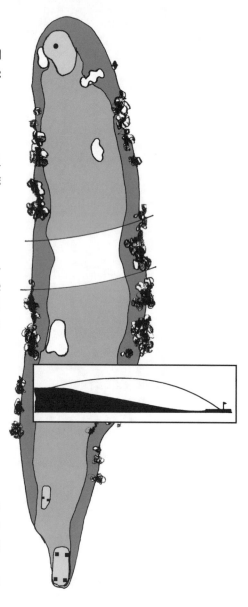

DRILL:

The purpose of this drill is to accentuate an inside take away of the club while keeping the club low to the ground. Place a club on the ground parallel to but approximately two to three inches beyond the target line and one to one and one-half feet behind the ball with th(grip end facing the target (see photo b). Focus on makin; long, slow backswing, keeping the club head close to ground to a point slightly beyond the end of the grip fa the target.

Full Swing to a Green Below

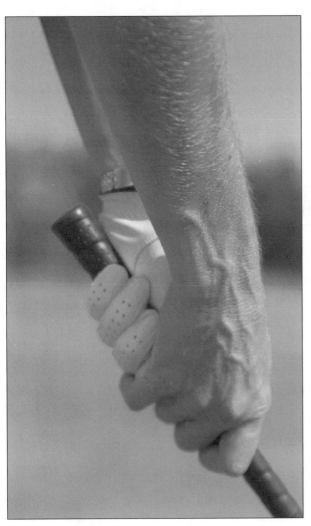

a

b

TIP: If you continue to hit high slicing shots, then practice by placing a tee in the ground six inches behind the ball and in your ideal swing path. Then, with your eyes closed, take the club back as one piece. If you are on the right backswing path with the club still moving low to the surface, you should gently clip the tee from the ground.

19 Downhill Lie

> **SITUATION:** A full shot from a downhill lie on an undulating fairway to a green at a distance of 180 yards to 225 yards. The green is narrow but deep, with a depth of 40 yards from front to back.

STRATEGY:

This situation requires a left-to-right shot of long distance but with sufficient trajectory. The left-to-right curving shot is required because the slope forces an outside-to-inside swing path.

TECHNIQUE:

The setup for this shot is an open stance (see situation 5, page 18) that requires two adjustments from the basic stance: (1) move the ball position three to four inches back in the stance and (2) align your shoulders, hips, and knees parallel to the slope (see photo a).

CONCEPT:

A natural tendency in this situation is to pull out of the swing in the impact area, resulting in a shot that is sculled, low, and to the right. The challenge is to begin the shot on the correct line and allow the setup and loft of the club to produce a high, soft fade.

DRILL:

Find a moderate slope (you may need to ask permission from a golf professional at a course) that allows you to adjust your ball position and posture to the correct technique. Place a tee in the ground four to five inches in front of the ball on the correct target line, which is aimed to the left side of the green. Swing through the ball, attempting to clip the tee from the ground and keeping the back of your forward hand facing the sky until the club has reached waist height (see photo b).

a

b

TIP: Try to feel as though the club follows the slope for about two feet after impact.

20 Uphill Lie

SITUATION: A shot from an uphill lie on an undulating fairway to a green at a distance of 180 to 225 yards.

STRATEGY:

Hit a full, straight shot, taking advantage of the increased launch angle created by the incline of the hill.

TECHNIQUE:

Because of the increase in the launch angle provided by the slope, use one more club than you normally would for this situation. For example, use a 3 wood instead of a 4 or 5 wood. Then, set your weight slightly (approximately two-thirds) to the uphill side and align your knees, hips, and shoulders with the slope (see photo a). Moving the ball slightly back to the middle of the stance will help you to reduce your tendency to pull up on the shot at impact.

CONCEPT:

Because of the difficulties associated with shifting your weight uphill in this situation, you will use your arms more and lower body less than when making a fairway wood shot from a flat lie. To compensate for this difficulty and to keep the shot on the correct target line, use a slightly closed stance (see situation 6, page 20).

DRILL:

The purpose of this drill is to help you resist the temptation to help the ball up into the air by altering your posture angle at the moment of impact. Use two and three-quarter inch tees and begin with the basic stance (see photo a). Attempt to hit the ball cleanly off the tee while at the same time retaining your posture angle. Hit 5 or 10 balls at this height, then repeat this sequence three times, reducing the height of the tee by one-half inch each time. Complete the drill by placing the ball directly on the ground and swinging through without producing a divot until after contacting the ball.

a

TIP: If you continue to have difficulty making solid contact with the ball, focus on feeling your shoulders rotating in a plane parallel to the target line.

21 Sidehill Lie Above Your Feet

> **SITUATION:** The ball is in the fairway but lying on a sidehill slope at a level substantially above your feet. The shot is 180 to 225 yards to a green guarded heavily by bunkers on the left side.

STRATEGY:

To compensate for the natural flight of the ball to the left (for a right-handed person the flight will be away from the slope of the hill), hit a shot that holds its line and does not curve excessively to the left.

TECHNIQUE:

Stand slightly more erect than you would with a normal lie and adjust the ball position to the middle of the stance. Depending on the degree of slope, choke down one to two inches on the club to compensate for the relative proximity of the ball created by the lie (see photo a). Balance your weight comfortably into the hill on the balls of your feet (see photo b).

CONCEPT:

Because the flight of the ball will naturally curve to the left off this type of sidehill lie, you must aim the ball approximately 10 yards farther to the right of the target than normal. By standing more erect to the shot and placing the ball closer to the middle of the stance, you can minimize the curve.

DRILL:

Use extra-long golf tees (about two and three-quarters to three inches long) to simulate an above-the-feet lie and to practice controlling the height and arc of your swing path. Practice until you can vary the heights of the ball and tee while consistently making solid contact.

Sidehill Lie Above Your Feet

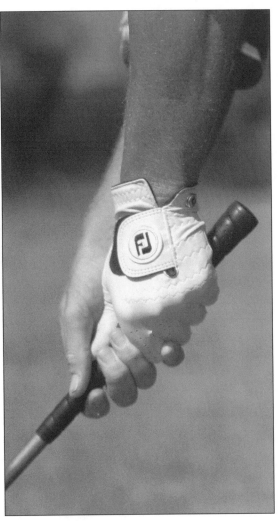

a

b

TIP: This swing should feel less vertical and more rounded than most other swings. Try to feel as though your shoulders are turning in a somewhat more level plane as they would when swinging a baseball bat.

22 Sidehill Lie Below Your Feet

SITUATION: The ball is in the fairway, but resting on a sidehill slope at a level below your feet. The shot to the green is at a distance of 180 to 225 yards.

STRATEGY:

To compensate for the natural flight of the ball to the right (for a right-handed person the flight will be away from the slope of the hill), make a solid shot that starts the ball slightly to the left of the target but then falls to the right without excessive slicing.

TECHNIQUE:

Modify your stance to achieve balance by placing more weight on your heels and increasing the bend at your knees. Use one more club than you normally would for the situation. For example, use a 4 wood instead of a 5 wood. Adjust the ball closer to the middle of your stance (see photo a).

CONCEPT:

Maintaining balance and the posture just described during the swing will help to control the swing path and minimize the natural curved flight of the ball to the right (see photo b). Focus on maintaining this stance to avoid distorting the shot by either pulling away from the ball or leaning excessively into the ball.

DRILL:

The purpose of this drill is to learn to maintain the same posture throughout the swing. Use the basic stance (see situation 1, page 10) and normal posture to make practice swings at a tee. Do not, however, look at the tee. Instead, focus your vision on a landmark at eye level in front of you, at a tree or fence, for example. Then swing, allowing the club to brush the tee as the club moves through the impact area. By concentrating on a distant target rather than the ground below, this drill encourages you to feel the tilt at your waist and the flex in your knees during the swing.

a

b

TIP: To counteract the tendency to throw your club at the ball and to avoid excessively activating your hands and arms, try to feel your left shoulder (for a right-handed person) move under your chin on the backswing and your right shoulder move under your chin during the forward swing. This approach will produce the sense of a more vertically oriented swing.

23 Controlled Hook

SITUATION: A shot from a fairway with a slight dogleg to the left and lined by trees on the left side. The green is at a distance of 180 to 225 yards, and the pin is positioned in the middle of the green but to the left side.

STRATEGY:

Hit a controlled hook shot that follows the contour of the fairway to the hole, curving from right to left by 15 to 20 yards. This strategy eliminates the need to skirt the corner of the dogleg or to fly the trees to land the ball on the green.

TECHNIQUE:

Use a closed stance (see situation 6, page 20) and move the ball back one to one and one-half inches in the stance (see photo a). Begin with about two-thirds of your weight on the back foot. Slightly close the club face behind the ball by moving the toe of the club slightly toward the ball.

CONCEPT:

Because shots that hook 15 to 25 yards usually will roll considerably after landing, the objective for this situation is to produce a shot with sufficient height and trajectory to offset the roll when the ball reaches the green (see photo b).

DRILL:

Use the closed stance with two-thirds of your weight to the right side. Position the ball one to one and one-half inches to the middle of the stance. Stand with your back nine inches to one foot from a wall. Make your backswing and pause at the top; on your forward swing, try to keep the club in contact with the wall until your hands reach waist height. The objectives of this drill are to maintain more weight behind the ball at the moment of impact and to ensure an inside-to-square club path. Maintaining your weight behind the ball substantially increases the launch angle at impact.

Controlled Hook

a

b

> **TIP:** If you continue to slice or hit the ball straight, try to feel as though your hands are falling behind you during the forward swing.

24 Controlled Slice

SITUATION: From a fairway with out-of-bounds lining the left, a shot to a green at a distance of 180 to 225 yards. The green is guarded heavily by bunkers on the left; the back of the green also borders an out-of-bounds.

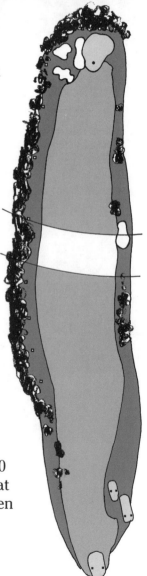

STRATEGY:

Hit a controlled slice that works away from the trouble on the left and has sufficient distance to land softly on the green. Because a left-to-right shot tends to land more softly with reduced roll, a controlled slice is preferred for working away from trouble on the left.

TECHNIQUE:

Use an open stance with an angle of 25 to 30 degrees to the left of the intended target line (see situation 5, page 18) and with even weight distribution at setup. Position the ball one to one and a half inches forward in the stance and maintain the club face square to the original target line (see photo a).

CONCEPT:

This shot offers the greatest degree of control, is one of the easiest to hit under pressure, and minimizes the risk of incurring a penalty stroke.

DRILL:

Find a tree approximately 80 feet tall. From a distance of about 200 yards from the tree, practice hitting full 3-, 4-, or 5-wood shots that begin just to the left side of the tree, rise to tree-top height, and then curve around to fall to the right of the tree (see photo b).

a

b

TIP: If you pull this shot to the left or consistently hit it straight, then try keeping your forward hand and wrist firm and flat, and delay as long as possible any rotation of your forward arm through the impact zone.

25 Fairway Bunker

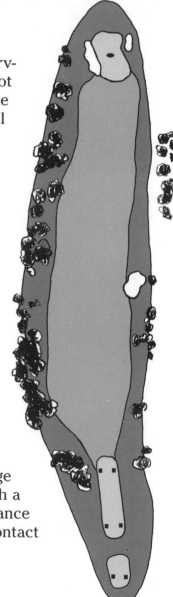

STRATEGY:

Hit a solid shot by picking the ball cleanly off the sand and curving the flight of the ball from left to right. Because you cannot ground your club in a bunker or hazard, the nature of the take away is an upright and outside-to-inside swing path that will produce a shot moving from left to right.

TECHNIQUE:

Use the open stance (see situation 5, page 18) to produce an outside-in swing path. Move the ball back to the middle of the stance and work your feet comfortably into the sand to ensure optimal balance.

CONCEPT:

This shot requires a steady base, a swing that lifts more vertically to eliminate any possibility of contacting the sand during the backswing, and a more steeply descending angle of attack on the forward swing. The resulting outside-to-inside swing path produces a natural left-to-right shot.

DRILL:

Use a shallow bunker for practice. Place 20 to 30 striped range balls in the bunker with the stripes horizontal and each with a clean lie resting on top of the sand (see photo a). Using the stance just described, focus on hitting each ball on the stripe to contact the ball cleanly with little or no divot.

a

TIP: Try to keep your hands ahead of the club face well past the point of impact.

Hale Irwin:
Master of Long Irons

Hale Irwin sets the standard for long-iron mastery in mens professional golf. Among Irwin's peers, he is especially regarded for his ability to play the most difficult golf courses, as reflected by his three U.S. Open wins on Winged Foot in 1974, Inverness in 1979, and Medinah in 1990. Irwin's consistent control of both distance and accuracy distinguishes his long-iron shotmaking from other top players.

PGA Tour stars have noted that Irwin's swing is exceptionally natural and rhythmic—critical requirements for the effective use of long irons. His perfect tempo and balance produce the solid contact necessary for shots of consistent distance and pinpoint accuracy. Irwin is not known for spectacular shots such as those by the likes of Jones, Palmer, and Nicklaus; instead, because of his remarkable ability to repeatedly place long-iron shots in birdie range, he stands beside Ben Hogan, Byron Nelson, and other legendary ball strikers. Hale Irwin's long-iron mastery has enabled him to build and maintain a complete game, leading to sustained success on the Senior PGA Tour.

An Academic All-American at the University of Colorado, Hale Irwin was the 1967 NCAA golf champion and played cornerback for the football team. Irwin's lifetime earnings as a member of the PGA Tour and Senior PGA Tour top $9 million. In 1996, he was the Senior Tour scoring leader (at an average of 69.5 strokes per round), and also lead in numbers of greens in regulation, numbers of birdies, and in the all-around category. He once played 86 consecutive Tour events without missing the cut!

© GolfStock/Keiichi Sato

Chapter 4

Long Irons

This chapter addresses situations inviting the use of long irons, the forgotten clubs in the modern golf bag. The long irons (1, 2, and 3 irons) are neglected for two reasons. First, because new technologies have produced higher-lofted fairway woods (5, 6, and 7 woods), many golfers have shunned the long irons. Second, because long irons are difficult to use, many amateur golfers have lost patience and abandoned these clubs. For you to achieve complete mastery of the long game, however, you must learn how to use these clubs effectively. In addition, mastering the long irons will help you improve the basic ballstriking skills you need for all clubs, and will increase your options and skills for coping with a variety of difficult situations.

The first group of situations in this chapter (situations 26-28) covers the use of long irons from the tee box on par-4 and par-5 holes, and for the rarely practiced lay-up shots on par-5 holes. The drills and techniques included for these situations will help you to attain the rhythm, timing, and sustained wrist cock necessary for proper play with long irons. The second group (situations 29-31) addresses the use of long irons for second-shot approaches to par-5 holes and for making curving shots (controlled-hook and slice shots). The final group (situations 32-36) covers the use of the long irons from bunkers and uneven lies on the fairway—including shots from uphill, downhill, and sidehill lies with the ball above or below the feet. The drills included for these situations will help you increase your confidence by making the ideal adjustments to setup and will help you master proper posture, swing plane, and balance.

26   Tee Shots on Par 4s and 5s

> **SITUATION:** A tee shot on a par-4 hole at a distance of 365 yards. The left of the fairway is lined by out-of-bounds the entire length of the hole, while a water hazard borders the right beginning at a distance of 220 yards. The width of the fairway is 40 yards from tee to green.

STRATEGY:

The ideal tee shot eliminates from play as many of the potential hazards as possible. Because the width of this fairway is about twice that of most greens, a 2- or 3-iron shot allows use of a free swing from the tee and leaves only a short-iron second shot to the green.

TECHNIQUE:

This shot requires the basic stance (see situation 1, page 10).

CONCEPT:

Make a full, free swing without guiding the shot to avoid the hazards on both sides of the fairway. Because of the fairway's width, even a poor shot will leave the ball in play with an open shot to the green.

DRILL:

One key to using long irons effectively is to maintain proper rhythm and tempo; therefore, this drill's purpose is to help you focus on the rhythm of the swing. Use the technique described above and place a metronome set at 76 beats per minute nearby. Swinging at the cadence of the metronome, try to simulate the feeling of a waltz tempo (1-2-3, 1-2-3), in which beat 1 corresponds to your backswing (see photo a), beat 2 to the transition to the forward swing (see photo b), and beat 3 to the finish position (see photo c).

Tee Shots on Par 4s and 5s

26

a

b

c

TIP: If you have difficulty maintaining a consistent rhythm for your swing from a stance of full width, then narrow your stance until your heels are nearly touching and resume practicing. Progressively widen your stance until you find the width at which you begin to speed up your swing. Continue hitting from that stance until you can maintain your rhythm. Repeat this approach until you reach the full width of your basic stance.

27 Tee Shots on Par 3s

SITUATION: A tee shot to a par 3 hole at a distance of 175 to 205 yards. The pin is placed on the front of a double-terraced green with a depth of 35 yards.

STRATEGY:

Because the average distance variation of consecutive irons is from 6 to 10 yards, the use of a long iron in this situation allows you to make a full swing while controlling the distance of your shot with greater precision than you can with a fairway wood.

TECHNIQUE:

Use the basic stance (see photo a).

CONCEPT:

The primary benefits of using long irons for tee shots on long par-3 holes are accurate control of distance and increased odds of leaving you in proximity to the pin. In addition, even poor tee shots leave you having to make only relatively short pitches, chips, or bunker shots. In many cases, these shots are excellent birdie opportunities.

DRILL:

Golfers frequently attempt to overswing their long irons, thereby causing an early release of their hands and club head in the impact area. Learning to maintain proper wrist cock well into the forward swing is essential for overcoming this tendency. Using the basic stance, place a club on the ground in front of your feet four to six inches from your toes and parallel to the target line (see photo b). Practice swinging very slowly, keeping your wrists fully cocked in the forward swing so the club lines up directly on top of the club on the ground. Your hands should be even with your right leg, your weight shifted to the forward foot, and your hips open 35 to 40 degrees. Repeat this swing four times and then hit a ball, trying to sustain the wrist cock as long as possible.

a

b

TIP: If you struggle to keep the club from hitting the ground before contacting the ball, then try feeling your right elbow make contact with your right hip for extra support during the transition from your backswing to forward swing.

28 Laying Up on Par 5s

> **SITUATION:** The second shot on a par-5 hole with a total distance of 525 yards. The width of the fairway is 40 yards but narrows to 25 yards near the green. The ball is approximately 275 to 300 yards from the green. In addition, several bunkers are located in the middle of the fairway 50 yards from the green.

STRATEGY:

The second shot should place the ball in the most advantageous position for the approach onto the green by eliminating the bunkers from play. Therefore, hit a 2 or 3 iron to a position short of the bunkers with a level lie and optimal angle to attack the pin.

TECHNIQUE:

Use the basic stance (see situation 1, page 10), but choke down one-half inch on the grip (see photo a). Choking down on the grip will increase control of both distance and accuracy in this swing.

CONCEPT:

Because most golfers cannot reach this par-5 green with the second shot, they believe the consequences of the shot to be minimal. This shot, however, demands careful planning of both distance and direction. The two principal objectives of this shot are to achieve a level lie and to place the ball a comfortable distance from the green for the third shot. The goal is to place the ball where you can reach the green with a short iron or a wedge.

DRILL:

This drill will help you develop proper timing and make solid contact using your long irons. First, use two clubs or other markers to establish parallel target and body lines. Then, depending on the surface (a mat or grass), use sidewalk chalk, spray paint, or a sharp stick to make a line perpendicular to the target and body lines at the normal position of the placement of the ball (see photo b). Try to make your club hit directly on the line or slightly to the target side (up to one inch forward).

a

b

TIP: If you want to learn to draw your long iron, you should attempt to feel the toe of your club making the initial contact with the ground or mat. If you are practicing fading your long iron, then attempt to feel the middle of the club face making contact with the ground or mat.

29 Going For It on Par 5s

SITUATION: A shot of 180 to 210 yards to the green of a relatively short par-5 hole with a total distance of 480 yards. The pin is set in the middle-left portion of a green guarded by bunkers to the front and left, and on the back right corner. The green is double tiered and has a depth of 35 yards.

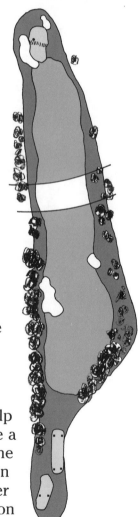

STRATEGY:

Because of the placement of the pin and bunkers, attack the front right portion of this green with a shot that will hold the green, thereby providing an opportunity for a putt for eagle and increasing dramatically the chances for a birdie.

TECHNIQUE:

You have the option of hitting either a fade shot (see situation 5, page 18) or a draw shot (see situation 6, page 20).

CONCEPT:

The approach to this situation requires either fading the shot to avoid the bunkers on the left or drawing the shot to use the open area on the right front portion of the green. Both of these shots will hold the green, leaving an easy chip or a putt of moderate distance.

DRILL:

This situation may induce hurried and sculled shots. This drill will help you hit long irons with sufficient trajectory to hold the green. Place a club on the ground perpendicular to the normal ball position in the target line and move your head three to five inches behind the club in the setup position (see photo a). As you swing, your front shoulder should pass the line created by the club and move under your chin on the backswing, ensuring full weight transfer (see photo b). During the forward swing, keep your chin (or nose) pointed to a position one to two inches behind the line until you connect with the ball.

a

b

TIP: If you continue to scull or otherwise mis-hit these shots, pause at the top of your backswing to ensure that lower-body movement begins the forward swing.

30 Sweeping Hook From the Fairway

SITUATION: A shot with a distance of 175 to 200 yards from the fairway to a large green with the pin set in the back left corner. The green is guarded heavily by bunkers on the front left and right rear.

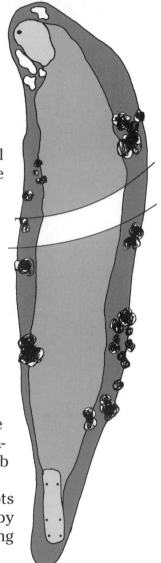

STRATEGY:

Remove the bunkers from play and exploit the opening of the green by hooking a 2- or 3-iron shot from right to left.

TECHNIQUE:

Use a closed stance (see situation 6, page 20) and position the ball one inch more toward the middle of the stance (see photo a). Close the club face slightly at address.

CONCEPT:

This approach allows you to curve the ball around the trouble and land the shot in the access corridor to the pin.

DRILL:

The purpose of this drill is to increase the shoulder turn of a closed stance, thereby exaggerating the inside swing path. Begin by placing a club on the ground parallel to the target line with the club face away from the ball and pointed toward you. Then touch your forward heel to the ball side of the club shaft and touch the toe of your back foot to the club face side of the shaft. Finally, separate your feet by a distance of 10 to 12 inches and close the club face slightly (see photo b).

Now hit 10 to 15 balls until you are consistently producing shots that hook 10 to 20 yards from the initial starting line. Follow this by hitting 10 to 15 balls using the normal closed stance and producing the same degree of hook.

Sweeping Hook From the Fairway

30

a

b

TIP: If you are unable to produce a sweeping hook shot, then relax your forward arm and hand to reduce any tendency to overguide the swing path.

31 Sweeping Slice From the Fairway

SITUATION: A shot with a distance of 175 to 200 yards from the fairway to a large green with the pin set in the back right corner. The green is guarded heavily by bunkers on the front right and left rear.

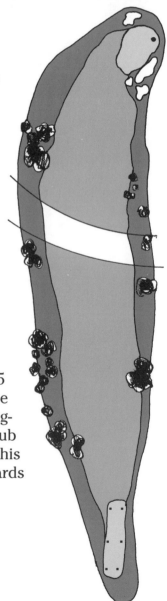

STRATEGY:

Remove the bunkers from play and exploit the opening of the green by slicing a 2- or 3-iron shot from left to right.

TECHNIQUE:

Use an open stance (see situation 5, page 18) and position the ball one inch more toward the front of the stance (see photo a). Open the club face slightly at address.

CONCEPT:

Because of the natural tendency to slice, this shot is always the easiest to hit under pressure, allowing you to curve the ball around the trouble and land it in the access corridor to the pin.

DRILL:

First, use a club to establish a target line to a fixed point 10 to 15 yards to the left of the pin. Then set the club face open on the ground behind the ball and open to the target line. With an exaggerated open stance of 30 to 40 degrees, practice swinging the club down the target line while leaving the club face open. Repeat this drill until you consistently produce a shot that slices 10 to 20 yards from the initial starting line.

Sweeping Slice From the Fairway

31

a

b

TIP: If you are unable to produce a sweeping slice shot, concentrate on keeping the back of your forward arm and hand facing the sky until the club has passed waist high in the forward swing (see photo b).

SITUATION: The ball is sitting cleanly on top of the sand in a shallow fairway bunker at a distance of 175 to 200 yards to the green.

STRATEGY:

Use the 3 iron to hit a fading shot that moves from left to right with a high degree of spin and moderate trajectory. Because you cannot ground your club in a bunker, the nature of the take away is an upright and outside-to-inside swing path that will produce a shot moving from left to right.

TECHNIQUE:

Use an open stance with normal width (see situation 5, page 18), but position the ball one to two inches toward the middle of the stance. Plant your feet firmly in the sand with two-thirds of your weight to the forward foot and set your hands slightly ahead of the ball.

CONCEPT:

In contrast to a wood, a long iron in this situation affords more precise control of distance and additional loft.

DRILL:

The purpose of this drill is to develop both a feel and the technique for picking the ball cleanly off the surface of the sand. The ideal practice surface at the driving range is a spot of bare ground or an extremely hard mat. At the beach, try wet and firm sand. Take a slightly open stance and position the ball one to two inches toward the middle of the stance. Practice making punch shots from a three-quarter backswing (see photo a) to a three-quarter forward finish, focusing on hitting the ball first (see photo b).

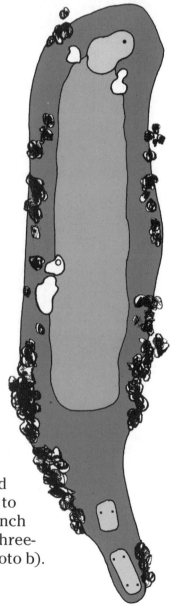

a

b

TIP: If you tend to pull or pull-hook these shots, be certain to set your hands ahead of the ball at address. Notice the angle and depth of divots and do not allow the toe of the club to pass the heel until the club reaches the knee-high position in the forward swing.

33 Downhill Lie to a Long Par 4

SITUATION: A second shot from a downhill lie on a moderately sloping fairway to a green at a distance of 175 to 210 yards. The green is guarded by a bunker on the right front and back left.

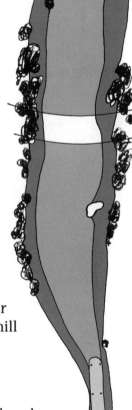

STRATEGY:

Hit a left-to-right curving shot, removing the bunkers from play and landing the ball on the front left, center, or back right of the green.

TECHNIQUE:

Adapt the open stance (see situation 5, page 18) to the severity of the slope by moving the ball three to four inches back and aligning your shoulders, hips, and knees parallel to the slope.

CONCEPT:

Due to the downhill slope, ball position and aim during the setup of the shot are especially important. Complete the backswing to avoid pulling up and away from the ball at impact, thereby hitting the ball off-line.

DRILL:

Practice these drills at both the driving range and the golf course. The range drill simulates a downhill lie to help you practice proper weight transfer and balance. The on-course drill uses natural downhill lies to help you establish proper setup and practice aiming.

RANGE DRILL:

Use the setup described in the technique. Tilt your body downward by placing a telephone book under your back foot. Practice making full shoulder turns—turning your back completely to the target—and transferring your weight in both the back and forward swings (see photos a and b).

Downhill Lie to a Long Par 4

ON-COURSE DRILL:

During a practice or casual round of golf, practice your setup (that is, ball position) and alignment. Vary the position of the ball toward the back of your stance while you hit three to four balls until you have discovered the correct combination of ball position, posture, and open stance. Continue to practice these drills at the driving range and golf course until you can confidently produce a consistent trajectory and ball flight curve to the target.

a

b

TIP: If you continue to hit thin or off-line shots, then focus on keeping your back shoulder moving down the slope to the finish position.

34 Uphill Lie to a Long Par 4

> **SITUATION:** Second shot from the fairway at a distance of 165 to 195 yards to the green. The lie is at the base of a long upslope to a green that is bunkered in the front but open in the back.

STRATEGY:

Because the sloping lie will add natural loft to this shot, the trajectory will resemble that of a ball struck by a 4 or 5 iron. Therefore, use a longer club, a 2 or 3 iron, and play the shot to the middle or back of the green.

TECHNIQUE:

Set your weight approximately two-thirds to the front (uphill) side of the stance, and align your knees, hips, and shoulders with the slope. Move the ball one to two inches toward the middle of your stance.

CONCEPT:

Most golfers fail to adjust adequately for the effect of the slope. As a result, their shots are generally short and off-line.

DRILL:

Practice these drills at both the driving range and the golf course. The range drill simulates an uphill lie to help you practice proper weight transfer and balance. The on-course drill uses natural uphill lies to help you establish proper setup and practice aiming.

RANGE DRILL:

Use the setup described in the technique. To tilt your body forward by placing your front foot on a telephone book (see photo a). Practice making full shoulder turns—turning your back completely to the target—and transferring two-thirds of your weight to the back foot. To swing, concentrate on transferring your weight as far onto the front (or uphill) foot as you can (see photo b)

34

ON-COURSE DRILL:

During a practice or casual round of golf, practice your setup (that is, ball position) and alignment. Vary the position of the ball toward the middle of your stance while you hit three or four balls until you discover the correct ball position and posture. Practice these drills at the driving range and golf course until you can confidently produce a consistent trajectory and ball flight curve to the target.

a

b

35 Sidehill Lie Above Your Feet

SITUATION: A shot of 175 to 200 yards to a large sloping green. The green is guarded by bunkers in the front and to the left side.

STRATEGY:

Hit a shot that curves from right to left into the middle of the putting surface by using the slope of the hill, the open side of the green, and the ease by which a long iron will curve a shot.

TECHNIQUE:

Stand slightly more erect than you would with a normal lie and adjust the ball position toward the middle of the stance one-half to one inch. Balance your weight into the hill on the balls of your feet. Choke down slightly to compensate for being closer to the ball.

CONCEPT:

Most golfers tend either to overcompensate or to completely disregard the effect of the sidehill slope on the shot. Taking advantage of this lie requires only a moderate adjustment in your aim and positioning of the ball.

DRILL:

Place two telephone books under your toes to shift your weight toward your heels (see photo a). Use extra-long golf tees (length of about two and three-quarters to three inches) or long rubber driving range tees to simulate an above-the-feet lie. Aim at a yardage sign, flag, or other landmark at a minimum distance of 175 yards. Vary the height of the ball while working on making consistent, solid contact that curves the ball 10 to 20 yards from the original target line.

a

> **TIP:** If your shots are curving excessively or are landing wide of the target, check the ball position. Excessive curve indicates the ball has not been moved back sufficiently, while too little curve indicates the ball has been moved back too far.

36 Sidehill Lie Below Your Feet

STRATEGY:

Using a long iron in this situation allows a controlled, balanced three-quarters swing that will produce a shot with reasonable spin that curves moderately away from the hill and toward the green.

TECHNIQUE:

Set up in a slight crouch with your weight evenly distributed over the heels of both feet. To assist you in maintaining good posture in this situation, use a slightly longer club, for example, a 3 iron instead of a 4 or 5 iron, or a 2 iron instead of a 3 or 4 iron. Position the ball one to two inches slightly toward the middle of the stance.

CONCEPT:

The primary considerations for this situation are control of distance, trajectory, and curve. The use of a long iron maximizes your ability to control these factors.

DRILL:

The purpose of this drill is to help you to learn to maintain proper posture and balance when swinging at a ball on a lie below your feet. Place two telephone books of moderate thickness, about two inches thick, under both feet to raise the level of your feet relative to the ball (see photo a). Hit balls by focusing on your posture and balance as described above (see photo b).

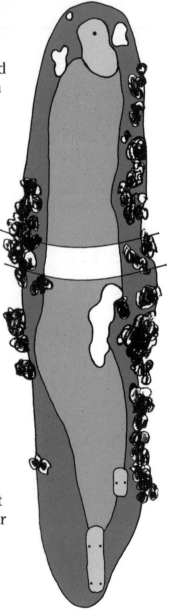

Sidehill Lie Below Your Feet

a

b

TIP: If you have difficulty maintaining your posture during impact, place a penny two to three inches in front of the ball and try to move the penny after impact with the ball.

© GolfStock

Jack Nicklaus:
Overcoming Conditions

In the final round of the 1972 U.S. Open Championship at Pebble Beach, Jack Nicklaus stood on the tee of the 17th hole knowing that he needed a strong finish in order to win this prestigious championship. The weather conditions for Pebble were typical: Nicklaus had to contend with near gale-like winds from the Pacific Ocean, while readying for a difficult shot to a tight pin placement in the back left corner of the storied par 3. Guarding the front of the green lay a foreboding sandtrap of gargantuan proportions which promised a bogey. To the left and rear of the green was the Pacific Ocean; but landing the ball on the right side of the multitiered green offered only a slim chance for par.

Under normal circumstances, Nicklaus would have used a 4 iron for this shot. However, because of the extenuating conditions, he selected his 1 iron. Into the teeth of the wind he launched a shot that bore directly toward the flag with the accuracy of a laser; for a moment, the force of the wind suspended the ball in the sky before releasing it to the green, where it struck the base of the flag before coming to rest only six inches from the cup. Once again, Nicklaus' abilities to correctly assess the conditions, select the right club, and hit a spectacular long-iron shot in a major championship captivated the golfing world and secured victory for him in another major.

Chapter 5

Strategies for Par 5s

The preceding four chapters have emphasized the development of skills you need for managing ballstriking situations on most golf courses. This chapter adapts the ballstriking skills you have learned in the preceding chapters and matches them to the fundamental strategies required for successfully negotiating par-5 holes. For at least three reasons, most amateur and recreational golfers fail to maximize their opportunities for birdies on par-5 holes. These reasons include a total absence of strategy, a poor strategy (for example, a high handicapper attempting to overpower a par-5 hole by trying shots beyond his or her capability), or a lack of knowledge regarding the terrain, hazards, out-of-bounds, or other key information needed for club selection and strategy.

The first group of situations in this chapter (situations 37-39) outlines approaches for exploiting the potential benefits of hills, valleys, moguls, and cart paths. By using the correct strategy, you can benefit from these features. The second group (situations 40-42) covers extreme situations, including island greens, long par 5s, and severely sloping fairways. The drills and strategies described for this group will help you avoid the normal pitfalls induced by these conditions, including attempting to hit shots to distances beyond your capabilities, becoming too aggressive (or too timid) when you are confronted by water hazards, and curving the ball incorrectly to a severely sloping fairway. The final three situations (situations 43-45) cover the average par 5, the reachable par 5, and the "sucker" par 5, and provide drills to increase your birdie opportunities while helping you avoid bogies and penalty shots.

37 Hills and Valleys

SITUATION: A tee shot to a fairway with severe undulations and a limited number of flat, intervening areas.

STRATEGY:

Select the right club for hitting your ball to a resting spot on one of the few flat areas.

TECHNIQUE:

Depending on the need for a straight shot, fade, or draw, use the appropriate basic stance (see situations 1, 5, and 6, pages 10, 18, and 20).

CONCEPT:

Hills and valleys will distort your perception of distance over fairways. All golf courses, however, set tees for such fairways so that players of all levels can reach flat areas comfortably with their tee shots. Because one of your basic shots always has the potential to find level ground, avoid the temptation to overswing or underswing.

DRILL:

To improve your perception of golf course distances, stand on a tee box and select a point of reference—an upright distance marker, tree, or top of a hill (see photo a). Record your estimate of the distance to that point and then measure the distance by walking to it from the tee. Alternatively, make a game of this with your playing partners.

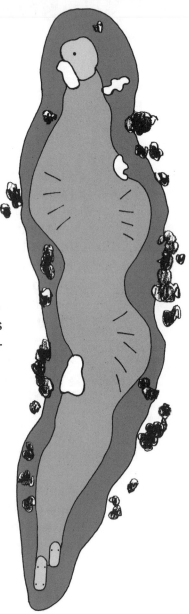

a

TIP: Calibrate your stride by using sprinkler heads at the golf course and fixed distances in your home.

38 Extra Distance

SITUATION: Tee shot to a severely undulating fairway with hills and valleys. The fairway is lined by moguls on both sides to a distance of 300 yards.

STRATEGY:

Hit either a power fade or controlled draw shot that uses the slopes, moguls, or cart path to increase the distance.

TECHNIQUE:

To increase the angle of your tee shot, position yourself on either the extreme right-hand or left-hand side of the tee box (see photos a and b). Use the techniques for hitting a fade (see situation 5, page 18) or draw (see situation 6, page 20).

CONCEPT:

Combining your most effective curving shot, either a fade or draw, with the slopes of moguls or the fairway can extend the distance of a tee shot by 25 to 30 yards.

DRILL:

Use landmarks at the driving range—mounds or distance markers—as targets for exaggerated hooks and slices, called sling hooks and banana slices, respectively.

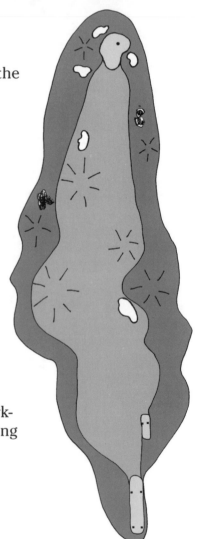

a

b

TIP: Learn to use clubs other than the driver for tee shots in this situation; vary your practice for tee shots by also using fairway woods and long irons.

39 Extra Control

SITUATION: A tee shot to a dogleg left par-5 hole lined by a steep slope and cart path on the right-hand side. A long downhill slope begins as the fairway turns left into the dogleg.

STRATEGY:

Hit a straight shot down the right side of the fairway using the right-hand slope as a backstop to either force the ball back into the fairway or keep the ball from running through the fairway and into trouble.

TECHNIQUE:

To maximize use of the width of the fairway and the slope on the right-hand side, increase the angle of your tee shot by positioning yourself on the extreme left-hand side of the tee box (see photo). Use the basic stance (see situation 1, page 10).

CONCEPT:

Although the usual temptation on a dogleg is to play down the short side of the hole closest to the dogleg to save yardage, this strategy often results in a completely blocked shot. The safest and smartest shot is to use the slope on the right-hand side and most of the fairway to keep the ball in play.

DRILL:

The objective of this drill is to become comfortable aiming tee shots at unusual angles. Use two clubs to establish a target line and body line and hit 10 balls at a specific target (see photo a). Then, select a new target to alter radically the target and body lines, up to 45 degrees from the previous lines. Hit 10 balls at this target (see photo b). Continue alternating targets until you are comfortable hitting at different angles.

a

b

TIP: If after setting your clubs and determining your correct alignment you continue to feel uncomfortable, then concentrate on keeping your feet steady and on maintaining your shoulder alignment. You should be able to see both shoulders from your peripheral vision whenever your shoulders are square to the target line.

40 Island Greens

STRATEGY:

To make par or better, play conservative shots in the fairway and incur no penalty strokes.

CONCEPT:

This situation actually represents two golf holes combined into one. The first is a par-4 distance of 420 yards, and the second, a par-3 of 100 yards. Avoid the temptation to play too aggressively on the first "par-4 hole." Playing more conservatively will help you avoid penalty strokes, awkward approaches, and putting yourself in between clubs. Then try to hit the green with your 8 or 9 iron or wedge.

DRILL:

To prepare for this situation, practice accuracy shots by hitting your driver, 3 wood, and 2 iron at a target the size of a blanket. For real play in this situation, use the clubs that produce the most accurate shots.

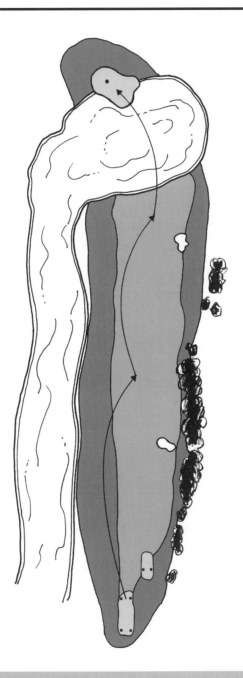

> **TIP:** Before each swing, take several deep breaths and attempt to visualize the target; then make as free a swing as you can.

41 Long Par 5s

SITUATION: A dogleg right par 5 at a distance of 580 yards. An out-of-bounds borders the entire right side of the fairway, and a lateral water hazard lines the left side from tee to green. The fairway is generous with a width of 50 yards.

STRATEGY:

Attempt only to put your drive into play and do not alter your natural shot.

TECHNIQUE:

Use the basic stance as appropriate and choose the side of the tee box affording you the maximum available angle to the target in the fairway.

CONCEPT:

Because the unusual total length of this hole may induce great anxiety, many golfers abandon their routine setups and swings. They attempt to hit shots to distances beyond their capabilities.

DRILL:

This is an on-course drill to teach you the concept of hitting the same club for varying distances and lies on long holes. On at least three consecutive rounds of golf, play the same long par 5 using your 2 iron for the tee shot, the second shot, and, if necessary, the third shot. By using a 2 iron for all shots on exceptionally long holes, you will learn to employ more effectively your distance capabilities and to improve your course management for such holes.

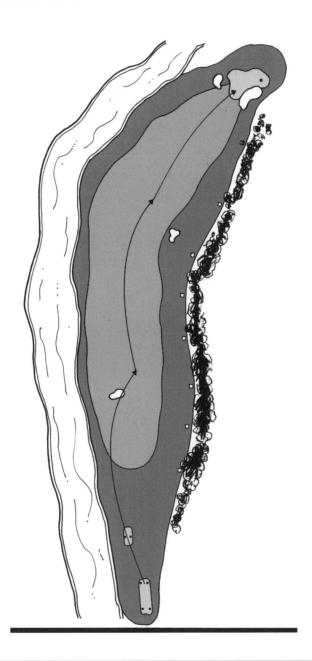

TIP: If you continue to overswing in situations such as this, focus on practicing and maintaining proper rhythm and tempo (see the drill in Situation 26, page 64).

 **Severely Sloping Fairways**

SITUATION: Tee shot to a par 5 with a fairway that slopes dramatically to the left or the right.

STRATEGY:

Minimize the effect of the slope on your ball once it hits the fairway by hitting a shot curving in the direction opposite the slope. For example, a right-handed golfer should hit a slice into a right-to-left slope.

TECHNIQUE:

Use open and closed stances as appropriate (see situations 5 and 6, pages 18 and 20).

CONCEPT:

Curving the ball into the slope controls the roll and ensures that the next shot can be in or close to the fairway.

DRILL:

Practice alternating 10 draw shots and 10 fade shots to the same target by varying only your stance.

Severely Sloping Fairways

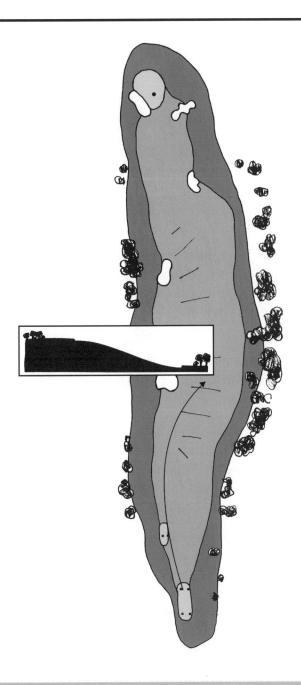

TIP: If you lose the ability to hit either a draw or a fade, then be certain the ball position is consistent with the shot you are attempting to hit (see situations 5 and 6, pages 18 and 20).

43 "Average" Par 5s

> **SITUATION:** A par-5 hole at a distance of 510 to 530 yards. Bunkers guard the landing area on both sides from 240 to 260 yards. Crossing bunkers appear 75 yards from the green. Bunkers guard the front left and back right of the green, which is 20 yards deep.

STRATEGY:

Bunker placement for this hole creates five options for primary landing areas. First select your landing area and then place your tee and second shots in the combination that will exploit your individual strengths—your distance capability or accuracy.

TECHNIQUE:

Use the technique that corresponds to your specific need to produce straight, draw, or fade shots (see situations 1, 5, and 6, pages 10, 18, and 20).

CONCEPT:

Most amateur golfers habitually hit their drivers and longest fairway woods on par-5 holes rather than selecting the most logical combination of long clubs based on the information provided by the club chart (see pages 4-5). Generate birdie opportunities and eliminate disasters by strategically using the club chart.

DRILL:

Use stationary objects (yardage signs, flags, fences, and other landmarks) to simulate 10 to 15 fairways and landing areas. Alternate between the driver, fairway woods, and long irons to determine the best combination of clubs for each hypothetical fairway and landing area. For example, use the driver and the 1 iron, the driver and the 4 wood, the 3 wood twice, the driver and the 3 wood, the 3 wood and the 5 wood, the driver and the 2 iron, and so forth.

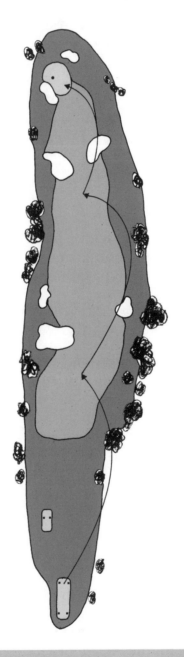

> **TIP:** Because range balls vary in quality, focus on the solidness of contact to develop confidence in each specific combination of clubs.

44 Reachable Par 5s

SITUATION: An inviting par-5 hole at a distance of 475 to 500 yards. The fairway is generous with a width of 40 to 50 yards and contains an isolated bunker on the right side at a distance of 230 yards. The green is large, open on the front, and guarded by bunkers only on the left side.

STRATEGY:

The generous fairway and near absence of hazards tilts the benefit-to-risk ratio for aggressive shotmaking in your favor. Therefore, be aggressive and aim for maximum distance with your tee shot.

TECHNIQUE:

To produce a tee shot with maximum distance, begin with two-thirds of your weight behind the ball (see situation 4, page 16).

CONCEPT:

The favorable conditions of this hole permit you to take more risks than usual and are conducive to recovery shots that will still allow opportunities for birdies and pars.

DRILL:

For this drill, you will need a steel reinforcing rod (approximately three feet long and five-eighths of an inch in diameter) mounted with a golf grip (see photo a). You can buy the rod at most hardware stores. Practice swinging the rod 15 to 25 times each day, accentuating the full shoulder turn and weight transfer in both the back and forward swings. Aim for the feeling of a late release of the club—a late release feels as though the rod reaches the bottom of the swing circle close to the forward foot (see photo b).

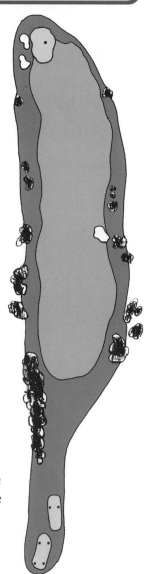

a

b

TIP: Concentrate on moving slowly through the transition of the swing from backward to forward, maintaining a full wrist cock as long as possible.

45 "Sucker" Par 5s

SITUATION: A par-5 dogleg left at a distance of 475 yards. Trees and bunkers line the left side of the fairway beginning at 225 yards, and a small pond fronts the multiterraced green.

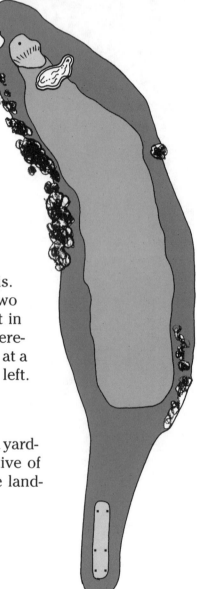

STRATEGY:

Hit your tee shot to the right center of the fairway rather than attempting to skirt the corner of the dogleg.

TECHNIQUE:

This shot requires a full swing and basic stance (see situation 1, page 10) but with approximately two-thirds of your weight set behind the ball on your back foot.

CONCEPT:

Because this hole doglegs, it appears even shorter than it is. The temptation is to cut the corner to reach the green in two shots. Attempts to cut the corner, however, usually result in bad lies that bring into play the pond and other trouble. Therefore, play this hole safely down the right and as though it is at a distance of at least 500 yards with an out-of-bounds on the left.

DRILL:

Establish an imaginary fairway with the aid of a landmark—a yardage sign, marker, or flag. Hit 15 tee shots with the objective of landing them in the imaginary fairway to the right of the landmark.

a

b

TIP: If you are hitting many of these shots to the wrong side of the fairway, then concentrate on feeling your arms maintain contact with your torso as they move through the impact position toward the finish (see photos a and b).

© UPI/Corbis—Bettmann

Gene Sarazen:
A Double-Eagle

The year was 1935. The event—The Masters. Craig Wood, popular Tour player, had retired to the hallowed clubhouse of the Augusta National Course confident that his final round had secured victory and already accepting congratulations from fellow competitors. But out on the fairway of the 15th hole—a treacherous but reachable par 5—the diminutive Gene Sarazen delicately gripped his 4 wood as he readied for his second shot. With four holes to complete, Sarazen knew he needed a string of birdies because he trailed Wood by a seemingly insurmountable 3 strokes. Sarazen checked the wind, adjusted his stance, and prepared himself completely for his attempt to reach the green in two. With unyielding nerve, he launched the second shot, hoping for an opportunity to make eagle and narrow the gap. To his delight, and to the shock of those few remaining spectators, the ball not only reached the green, but found its way into the bottom of the cup! Sarazen had made a double-eagle—the rarest of all shots in golf. With this one shot, he gained the momentum necessary to carry him through to a playoff and victory in a fashion comparable to Truman's come-from-behind win over Dewey.

Chapter 6

Creative Shotmaking

Most of the time, you will use the clubs featured in this book to hit shots in situations for which the clubs are primarily designed: drivers for hitting long shots from the tee box, fairway woods for making second shots on par 5s and par 4s, and long irons for standard shots on par 3s, par 4s, and par 5s. The design features of these clubs, however, also allow you to use them in a surprising variety of special situations. This chapter will help you become more creative and effective in using the driver, fairway woods, and long irons. Because of the special features of these clubs, they are suited for hitting several types of shots that generally seem to be unreachable—low shots to extricate yourself from wooded areas, curving shots necessary to maneuver around trees and other obstacles, and low boring shots that cheat the wind.

The situations in this chapter are organized into three basic categories. The chapter begins by describing special situations (situations 46-48) in which you can use the driver on either the fairway or from wooded areas. The second group of situations (situations 49-51) presents scenarios that teach you techniques for hitting shots over, under, or around obstacles using a combination of long irons and fairway woods. The last group of situations (situations 52-58) covers the use of these clubs for making shots from a variety of challenging surfaces and conditions, including light and heavy rough, bare ground, and strong winds.

46 "Hooking Driver" off the Fairway

> **SITUATION:** You have a 220- to 250-yard shot to the green of a par-4 hole at a total distance of 475 yards. The opening of the green is to the left side, and the green has a depth of 30 yards.

STRATEGY:

Long par 4s place a premium on distance shots. Because there are no obstacles on this hole, an effective low, hot hook produces the opportunity to putt for birdie.

TECHNIQUE:

Use the basic stance (see situation 1, page 10) with slightly more than half of your weight on the back foot. Move the ball to a position one inch farther to the back of the stance from normal and close the club face slightly (see photo a).

CONCEPT:

For most golfers, using the driver off the fairway can be risky and requires a perfect lie. Practicing this shot for such a situation can produce special rewards because few golfers can reach these greens in regulation.

DRILL:

This drill will help you develop proper timing and make solid contact using your driver from the fairway. First, use two clubs or other markers to establish parallel target and body lines (see photo b). Then, depending on the surface on which you are practicing (mat or grass), use a piece of sidewalk chalk, a can of spray paint, or a line of tees pressed into the ground at a height of a quarter inch to make a line perpendicular to the target and body lines and at the normal position of the placement of the ball (see situation 1, page 10). Take practice swings attempting to make your club hit directly on the line or remove the tees from the ground without hitting the ground first.

"Hooking Driver" off the Fairway

46

a

b

TIP: Relax your hands and allow yourself to feel the weight of the club head during the swing.

47 "Slicing Driver" off the Fairway

STRATEGY:

Because the green is not within range of the 3 wood, the driver can be used off the fairway in this situation. For this shot off the fairway, the reduced loft of the driver produces a natural left-to-right movement of the ball.

TECHNIQUE:

Use an open stance (see situation 5, page 18), but move the ball back one inch in the stance to ensure solid contact (see photo a).

CONCEPT:

This situation is optimal for "going for the green" with the second shot—the lie is perfect in the middle of a flat fairway with no obstructions. This shot maximizes both control and distance potential.

DRILL:

Using the technique just described, place a marker—for example, an umbrella or pole—40 yards in front of you (see photo b). Practice hitting balls that curve from left to right around the marker to a distant target.

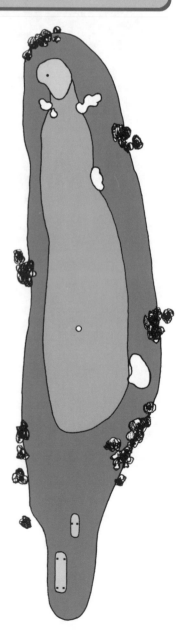

a

b

TIP: If you are pulling your shots or scattering them in different directions, check your body and target-line alignment and slow your backswing.

48 Driver From the Trees

SITUATION: The ball is resting in short rough or on bare ground amidst a cluster of trees at a distance of 190 to 210 yards to the green.

STRATEGY:

Hit a low shot from under the limbs that slices around the trees and carries 160 to 175 yards in the air before rolling onto the green.

TECHNIQUE:

Use an exaggerated open stance up to 40 degrees (see situation 5, page 18) and position the ball in the middle of the stance. Choke down one or two inches on the club (see photo a).

CONCEPT:

Although golfers often attempt to use a 2 or 3 iron in this situation, the ball frequently will hit overhanging tree limbs because of the loft produced by these clubs. The use of the driver in this situation will ensure that the ball remains low enough to escape the overhanging branches and still reach the green.

DRILL:

Practice this shot off bare ground or a hard mat at the driving range. Using the technique just described, concentrate on making solid contact and keeping the ball low for 15 to 30 yards.

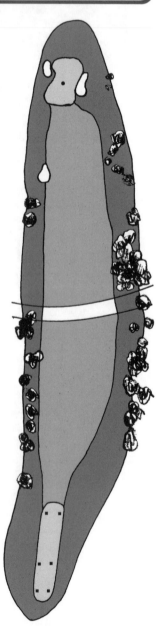

a

TIP: If initial contact with the ball produces excessive height for the situation, be certain that in the address position you keep about two-thirds of your weight on the forward foot.

49 Fairway Shot Over Trees

SITUATION: A shot from the left side of the fairway that must fly over a protruding small grove of trees to a green at a distance of 200 to 225 yards.

STRATEGY:

Use a 4 or 5 wood to hit a high, fading shot over the trees.

TECHNIQUE:

Use an open stance (see situation 5, page 18) with the ball placed one inch forward in the stance. Place approximately two-thirds of your weight on the back foot.

CONCEPT:

To achieve maximum trajectory, this shot requires a perfect lie. One of the few ways to reach the green in regulation is to use a high-lofted fairway wood. The outside-in swing path increases the launch angle and helps in adding height to this shot.

DRILL:

To achieve increased trajectory, you must retain a higher proportion of your weight behind the ball through the moment of impact. Use an open stance and the technique just described to practice hitting 4 and 5 woods. Keep your chin pointed to a position behind the ball well beyond impact and retain your posture angle as long as possible as you approach the finish position (see photo a).

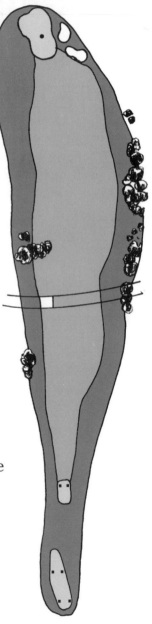

a

TIP: Maintain relaxation in your arms throughout the swing.

50 Low Hook

SITUATION: A shot from 15 yards behind a tree on the left side of a dogleg left fairway and at a distance of 165 to 185 yards to the green.

STRATEGY:

Hit a low hooking shot under the tree limbs, landing the ball within 20 yards of the green for a rollup onto the green.

TECHNIQUE:

Use a closed stance (see situation 6, page 20) and position the ball two inches to the back of the stance. Place approximately two-thirds of your weight on the forward foot and close the club face slightly (see photo a).

CONCEPT:

Because you are too close to the tree to hit over it, your primary objective is to hit the ball under and around this obstacle. A long iron, a 2 or 3 iron, is ideally suited to this shot because with it you can produce a hook or a slice and keep the ball low.

DRILL:

Place a marker, perhaps a trash can or golf bag, in front of you at a distance of 15 to 20 yards. Using the closed stance and technique just described, practice hitting punch shots—shoulder high to shoulder high (see photo b)—to curve the ball around the marker to a target in the distance.

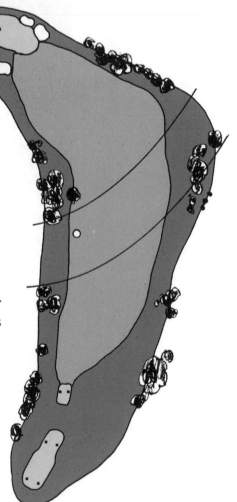

a

b

TIP: If your shots fail to curve sufficiently, concentrate on releasing your hands and arms through impact to a hook position. For example, your forearms should be touching at the waist-high position in the forward swing.

 **51** # Low Slice

SITUATION: The ball is 10 yards behind a tree on the extreme right side of the fairway and at a distance of 165 to 185 yards to the green.

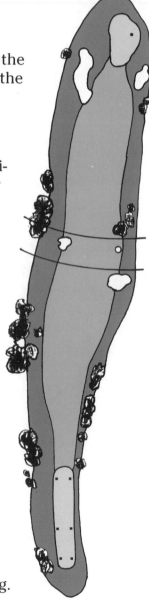

STRATEGY:

Hit a low running slice shot under the limbs of the tree, curving the ball back to the middle of the fairway and rolling it at least to the fringe of the green.

TECHNIQUE:

To achieve an exaggerated outside-in swing path, use a dramatically open stance (see situation 5, page 18) and place the ball far back in the stance, approximately two to three inches in front of the back foot.

CONCEPT:

In this situation, most golfers make the mistake of selecting their club based only on the distance to the green. As a result, they usually choose a club with too much loft for the situation. Use a less-lofted club, a 2 or 3 iron, to produce a shot with lower trajectory and sufficient distance to satisfy the additional yardage requirements of the curve.

DRILL:

Create a narrow opening by spacing two large trash cans (or other objects) at a distance of six to eight feet (see photo a). Using the exaggerated open stance just described, position yourself three to four yards behind the cans. Practice hitting balls through the opening and curving the shot back to a target in the distance (see photo b). Repeat this drill by adding five-yard increments of distance from the opening and make a record of the distance at which you fail to hit all your shots through the opening.

a

b

TIP: This swing should finish with the club barely beyond shoulder height.

52 Fairway Woods From Light Rough

SITUATION: The ball is resting in light rough at a distance of 190 to 215 yards from a large, multitiered green. The green is guarded heavily by bunkers in the front, and the pin is placed to the middle-right portion of the green.

STRATEGY:

Use a 3, 4, or 5 wood to play a high fading shot.

TECHNIQUE:

Use a slightly open stance (see situation 5, page 18) and position the ball one inch to the back. The club face should be slightly opened and your weight evenly distributed on both feet (see photo a).

CONCEPT:

Hitting a fairway wood normally requires a sweeping path at impact. A normal swing, however, usually fails in this situation because of interference by the longer grass. The result is a low, short shot; most golfers usually find that they are still in the rough after such shots. To overcome the interference of the longer grass, you need to alter your setup to achieve a slightly steeper backswing and a better angle of attack toward impact. Doing so will produce a more solid shot and high fade.

DRILL:

Use the modified open stance just described and place a club on the ground to establish a target line. Turn an empty soda can on its side and place it six to eight inches behind the ball. Practice hitting 10 to 15 balls with an increased wrist cock, attempting to make contact with the ball without touching the can (see photo b).

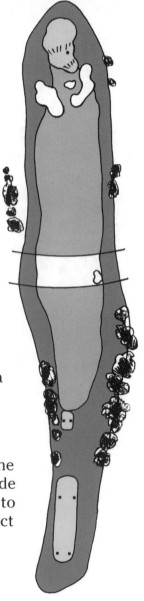

Fairway Woods From Light Rough

a

b

TIP: If during this drill you continue to clip the soda can on the downswing, then your swing path is still too shallow at impact. To increase your angle of attack in the forward swing, attempt to restrict your shoulder turn slightly during the backswing.

53 Long Irons From Light Rough

SITUATION: The ball is resting on top of light rough at a distance of 170 to 200 yards from a large green with a generous opening on the front and bunkers on the right middle and left rear.

STRATEGY:

Hit a long iron shot to the green, landing the ball on the front and allowing it to roll to the middle of the green.

TECHNIQUE:

Use a slightly open stance (see situation 5, page 18) and position the ball one inch to the back. The club face should be slightly opened and slightly more than half of your weight should be to the forward foot.

CONCEPT:

A long iron is the club of choice for this situation because the lie is too close for a full fairway wood. At the same time, the light rough may cause the ball to "fly" on impact, producing a shot slightly longer than normally expected.

DRILL:

Use a slightly open stance. Create two parallel lines of tees perpendicular to your target line. Each line should consist of about 10 tees spaced at three-inch intervals, and the two lines should be separated by four or five inches (see photo a). Practice swinging at the space between the two lines. Your divot should begin one to one and a half inches beyond the back line of tees and may remove some of the tees in the forward line. After you have mastered this drill, repeat the drill using balls placed two inches in front of the back row of tees; hit balls until you can make solid contact without hitting any of the back tees (see photo b).

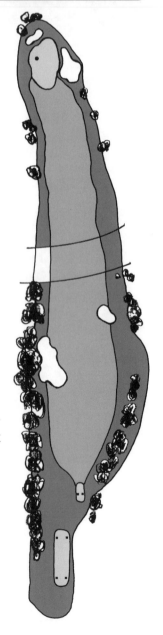

Long Irons From Light Rough

53

a

b

TIP: Focus on making an early wrist cock in the backswing and sustaining the wrist cock as long as possible in the forward swing.

54 Fairway Woods From Heavy Rough

> **SITUATION:** The ball lies 10 yards off the fairway nestled in the second cut of rough (three- to five-inch grass) at a distance of 175 to 200 yards to the green. The top of the ball is visible, indicating a lie as good as it gets in the long rough.

STRATEGY:

Use a high-lofted fairway wood (5 or 7 wood) to extricate the ball instantaneously from the grass and achieve maximum distance in this circumstance.

TECHNIQUE:

Use the open stance (see situation 5, page 18) and move the ball three to four inches toward the back foot. Choke down an inch and a half on the club and make an extremely upright backswing.

CONCEPT:

This situation frequently arises as the result of a mis-hit or an exceedingly aggressive tee shot. Many golfers make the mistake of using a 3 or 4 iron to solve this problem. Because the rough grabs the club face, however, the ball nose-dives back into the rough almost immediately. A higher-lofted wood (4, 5, or 7 wood) is more likely to cut through the grass and make contact cleanly, propelling the ball up and out of the grass and straight down the fairway.

DRILL:

This two-part drill will increase the steepness of the angle of attack to the ball. First, position yourself at arm's length plus the length of your club away from a wall or fixed object on your backswing side. Move four feet closer to the wall. Make a backswing that is barely clear of the wall. Begin your backswing focusing on an early wrist cock and a feeling of lifting your arms and hands to complete the backswing (see photo a). Second, place a soda can on its side six to eight inches directly behind the ball and in your swing path (see photo b). Using the technique just described, practice swinging at the ball by avoiding contact with the can and making clean contact.

Fairway Woods From Heavy Rough

a

b

TIP: Remember to grip the club firmly but maintain flexibility at the wrists.

55 Fairway Woods From a Hard Surface

SITUATION: The ball is sitting on a cart path at a distance of 180 to 225 yards to the green. An area of heavy rough lies to the right of the cart path, and a landscaped flower bed borders the left of the path.

STRATEGY:

Hit the shot directly off the cart path because there is no advantage to taking relief from the cart path in this situation.

TECHNIQUE:

Use a slightly open stance (see situation 5, page 18) and place the ball back one and one-half to two inches in the stance. Begin with two-thirds of your weight forward.

CONCEPT:

Most golfers become extremely anxious when faced with a golf ball resting on hard pan or on a cart path. In this situation, the nearest points of relief to either side of the path are poor choices and offer no immediate advantage over the cart path as a hitting surface. This solution increases your chances of making par in this difficult situation. In addition, learning to strike your ball cleanly off either of these surfaces will increase your confidence when playing from regular lies.

DRILL:

Practice this shot off sandy lies, bare ground, or a hard mat at the driving range (see photo a). Using the technique just described, concentrate on making solid contact and finishing your swing. This swing will have the feeling of hitting a punch shot with a fairway wood.

Fairway Woods From a Hard Surface

a

TIP: To ensure that the club head is always moving forward, swing as slowly as you can and focus on maintaining the angle of the wrist as long you can. This should feel as though the club head does not pass your hands until waist high in the follow-through.

56 Strong Headwind

SITUATION: A shot from the fairway at a distance of 200 yards to the green into a direct headwind of approximately 10 to 15 miles per hour. The green slopes from back to front and is 32 yards deep with bunkers on the left front and right rear.

STRATEGY:

Because a direct headwind will exaggerate the curve of any shot, hit as straight a shot as possible.

TECHNIQUE:

Modify the basic stance (see situation 1, page 10) by placing the ball in the middle of your stance. Begin the swing with two-thirds of your weight on the forward side.

CONCEPT:

Although the conditions of this situation call for a club with reduced loft, most golfers use a club with excessive loft. For example, at a distance of 200 yards to the target, they may hit a 5 wood when a 3 wood would be the correct choice. Minimize the tendency to overswing through proper setup and appropriate club selection.

DRILL:

Rather than avoiding direct headwinds for practice, be on the lookout for such conditions. Use them as opportunities to improve. When faced with a direct headwind, practice the following drill for 20 minutes. Set up using the technique just described. Begin with a 3 iron and hit a full driving shot into the wind. If possible, estimate and record the distance of your shot for the club. For example, you may record a shot of 175 yards for a 3 iron against a headwind instead of the normal distance of 200 yards. Repeat this drill with each club, maintaining a log of average distances for the different clubs under these conditions.

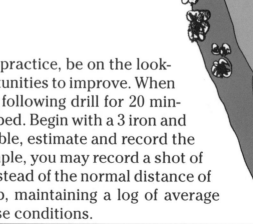

a

TIP: Focus on good tempo, solid contact, and passive hands. Stop your shoulder turn as it reaches the ball during the backswing (see photo a). Stopping the shoulder turn helps maintain proper weight distribution at the moment of impact by preventing excessive transfer of weight to the back foot.

57 Strong Tailwind

SITUATION: A tee shot on a par-5 hole heavily bunkered on both sides of the landing area at a distance of 230 to 260 yards from the tee. The width of the fairway in the landing area is 35 to 45 yards. The wind is blowing from behind at 10 to 15 miles per hour.

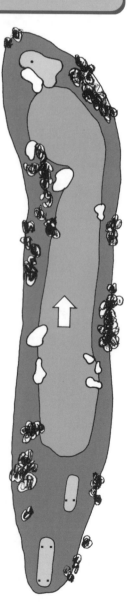

STRATEGY:

Place the ball in the fairway for maximum distance, knowing that playing downwind will minimize the curve of any shot.

TECHNIQUE:

Use the basic stance as modified for driving over water (see situations 1 and 3, pages 10 and 14). Use the normal stance and ball position but place two-thirds of your weight on your back foot (see photo a).

CONCEPT:

Many golfers attempt to curve this shot for additional distance but because the tailwind will minimize the curve, the ball is likely to land in the rough or a bunker. In addition, some golfers mistakenly expect the wind to carry the ball unreasonable distances—you should expect no more than a 10 percent increase in distance because of the wind. Therefore, avoid the temptation to make shots of unrealistic distances, for example, carrying bunkers at 260 yards.

DRILL:

On a day when the wind is at your back, use the technique just described to practice hitting high and solid drives. Estimate and record the distance of each shot so you can calculate an average distance for this condition. Because the ball is not likely to curve much, concentrate especially on aiming and playing a straight shot.

57

a

TIP: As you begin to achieve increased distances while practicing, focus on maintaining the same rhythm and tempo throughout the drill.

58

Combatting Crosswinds

> **SITUATION:** A tee shot on a 420-yard par-4 hole with a left-to-right wind blowing across the fairway. A lateral water hazard borders the right side of the fairway, and a series of three fairway bunkers line the left side of the landing area. The width of the fairway is 40 yards.

STRATEGY:

Hit either a straight shot down the left side of the fairway or a draw shot that holds its line against the wind.

TECHNIQUE:

Use either the basic stance (see situation 1, page 10) or the closed stance (see situation 6, page 20).

CONCEPT:

Instead of fighting the wind, aim the straight shot down the left side of the fairway, permitting the wind to gently push the ball toward the center. Alternatively, hit a draw shot down the center, allowing the opposite curve of the ball to hold the line and remain near the middle of the fairway.

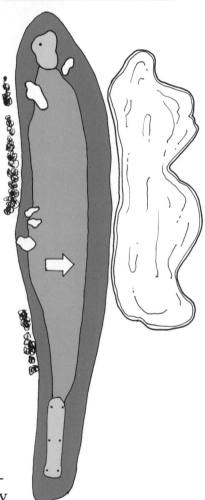

DRILL:

This drill will help you relax your swing while playing a shot in a crosswind; a narrower stance aids in producing good tempo and solid contact. Select a mat or practice tee situated between two yardage markers, target greens, or landmarks that simulate a fairway with a width of approximately 25 yards. Using a narrowed basic stance, with a heel separation of 10 to 14 inches, practice hitting shots down the left side of the simulated fairway (see photo a). Alternatively, using a narrowed slightly closed stance, practice hitting shots that begin down the middle of the fairway, then curve slightly to the left while remaining within the boundary of the simulated fairway.

a

TIP: Try to maintain the feeling of relaxed arms and sense the weight of the club head during the swing.

About the Authors

Daniel McDonald is head teaching professional at Hidden Valley Golf Center in Atlanta, Georgia, as well as head of golf instruction in the continuing education department at Dekalb College in Atlanta. He is also a former head professional at Atlanta's prestigious East Lake Country Club. In more than 18 years as a playing and teaching pro, McDonald has given more than 15,000 individual lessons. Although he seldom plays more than once a week, McDonald has remained competitive on mini-tours by using the drills in this book

For the past 12 years, McDonald has also conducted seminars on personal growth in which he demonstrates the need for skill development in order to achieve success.

Daniel McDonald lives in Clarkston, Georgia, with his wife, Jaquie. His leisure activities include meditation and dancing.

Richard A. Goodman, MD, MPH, is an author, manager, medical editor, and practicing physician at the Centers for Disease Control and Prevention in Atlanta.

His extensive writing and editing experience includes serving as editor of a well-known publication in the field of epidemiology; he has edited more than 2000 articles and has authored or coauthored more than 70 papers, chapters, and invited publications.

Dr. Goodman lives in Decatur, Georgia, with his wife, Deborah Kowal, his son, Zachary, and his daughter, Brooke. In his leisure time he enjoys spending time with his family, playing golf, and playing racquetball.

135

More great books for golfers from Human Kinetics!

Precision Wedge and Bunker Shots provides practical instruction and specific drills to help lower scores by mastering specific shots from 120 yards and closer to the green.

Fifty-three short-game situations and more than 100 photographs and 50 illustrations help readers visualize the required shot and learn how to execute it. Covers club selection, correct technique, basic course management, and drills for each situation. An excellent text for college golf classes and an essential resource for individual golfers and teachers.

**1998 • Paper • Approx 136 pp • Item PFIT0727
ISBN 0-88011-727-3 • $16.95 ($24.95 Canadian)**

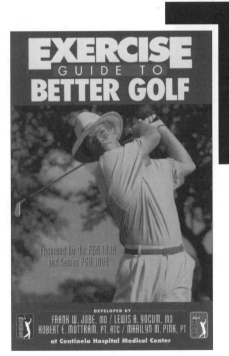

Endorsed by the PGA Tour and Senior PGA Tour

Frank W. Jobe, MD;
Lewis A. Yocum, MD;
Robert E. Mottram, PT, ATC;
Marilyn M. Pink, MS, PT

Exercise Guide to Better Golf shows readers how to perform the same muscle-strengthening and flexibility exercises top golfers on the PGA and Senior PGA tours use to get in shape and stay on top of their game. All of the exercises are easy to learn and have been designed specifically for golfers by Centinela Hospital Medical Center—official hospital of the PGA Tour and Senior PGA Tour.

**1995 • Paper • 92 pp • Item PJOB0893
ISBN 0-87322-893-6 • $9.95 ($14.95 Canadian)**

For more information or to place your order, U.S. customers call toll-free 1-800-747-4457. Customers outside the U.S. use the appropriate telephone number/ address shown in the front of this book.

HUMAN KINETICS
The Information Leader in Physical Activity
http:// www.humankinetics.com /

More great books for golfers from Human Kinetics!

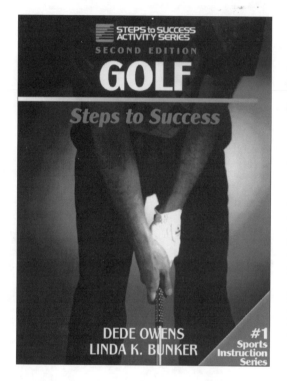

Golf: Steps to Success provides more than 80 drills and practice techniques to help golfers perform skills correctly and put them in practice out on the course.

Includes sequential lessons and 192 illustrations of proper form. The drills in the book come with performance goals and a list of key points to remember when performing each of them, and many include instructions for increasing or decreasing the difficulty of the drill.

1995 • Paper • 168 pp • Item POWE0578
ISBN 0-87322-578-3 • $14.95 ($21.95 Canadian)

In this second-level golf book, intermediate to advanced golfers climb 14 additional steps (chapters) to advanced golf success. This unique skill progression helps readers learn advanced swing techniques and strategies for controlling ball flight as well as attention and anxiety during competition.

With *Advanced Golf: Steps to Success*, readers will develop the skills necessary to become a low-handicap golfer, including drawing and fading the ball, options for sand play, off-green putting, variations in pitch shots, and much more.

1992 • Paper • 176 pp • Item POWE0464
ISBN 0-88011-464-9 • $15.95 ($22.95 Canadian)

HUMAN KINETICS
The Information Leader in Physical Activity
http://www.humankinetics.com/

For more information or to place your order, U.S. customers call toll-free 1-800-747-4457. Customers outside the U.S. use the appropriate telephone number/address shown in the front of this book.